DIANA LAFFIN

BRITISH SOCIETY since 1945

HODDER
EDUCATION
AN HACHETTE UK COMPANY

WAKEFIELD LIBRARIES

30000010269388

Dedication

I would like to dedicate this book to my mother, Dr Libby Wilson, who has set a wonderful example of what women can achieve.

The author and publisher wish to thank Dr Glen O'Hara for his patience, wisdom and invaluable advice as Academic Consultant.

Photo credits

Cover © Takaharu Yoshizawa/amanaimages/Corbis; **p.2** © Diana Laffin; **p.3** © Diana Laffin; **p.4** all © Diana Laffin; **p.5** © Diana Laffin; **p.6** *l* © Diana Laffin, *r* © Courtesy Everett Collection/Rex Features; **p.7** © f8 Imaging/Hulton Archive/Getty Images; **p.8** © Diana Laffin; **p.9** © travelib history/Alamy; **p.13** © Alistair Devine; **p.16** © Paul Doyle/Alamy; **p.18** *l* © itdarbs/Alamy, *r* © miroslavkaminski – Fotolia; **p.22** © Hulton Archive/Getty Images; **p.24** © Central Press/Getty Images; **p.25** © fotovika – Fotolia; **p.26** © Topham Picturepoint; **p.34** © So-Shan Au; **p.37** *l* © PA Photos/TopFoto, *r* © Press Association Images; **p.39** © Hulton-Deutsch Collection/Corbis; **p.40** *t* © Popperfoto/Getty Images, *b* © Roger Bamber/Rex Features; **p.43** *t* © Evening Standard/Hulton Archive/Getty Images, *b* © Keystone/Getty Images; **p.48** © Popperfoto/Getty Images; **p.49** © Science and Society/SuperStock; **p.53** © ITV/Rex Features; **p.54** © FremantleMedia Ltd/Rex Features; **p.55** © 2001 Topham Picturepoint; **p.64** © Harry Hammond/V&A Images/Getty Images; **p.65** © John Downing/Getty Images; **p.79** © W. Breeze/Evening Standard/Getty Images; **p.81** Cover Art Copyright © 1963 by Harlequin Enterprises Limited. Cover art used by arrangement with Harlequin Enterprises Limited. © and ™ are trademarks owned by Harlequin Enterprises Limited or its affiliated companies, used under license; **p.84** © Mander & Mitcheson Bristol University/ArenaPAL/TopFoto; **p.85** © Anglo-EMI/The Kobal Collection; **p.86** © Diana Laffin; **p.94** *t* © Ingram Publishing Limited, *b* © Deklofenak – Fotolia; **p.95** *t* © robograf/iStockphoto, *c* © Paul Turner – Fotolia, *b* © Maksym Yemelyanov – Fotolia; **p.105** *t* © Popperfoto/Getty Images, *b* © Richard Young/Rex Features; **p.112** *t* © 2001 Topham Picturepoint/TopFoto, *b* © Anwar Hussein/WireImage/Getty Images; **p.113** © PA Photos/TopFoto; **p.114** © BBC/Corbis; **p.116** © Mirrorpix; **p.123** © Gamma-Keystone via Getty Images.

Text credits

pp.28–29 Enoch Powell, extracts from 'I seem to see "the River Tiber foaming with much blood"', a speech given in Birmingham, 20 April 1968; **p.66** Philip Larkin, lines from 'Annus Mirabilis' from *Collected Poems*, edited by Anthony Thwaite (Faber & Faber, 1988), © the Estate of Philip Larkin, 1988; **p.70** Lesley A Hall, *Sex, Gender and Social Change in Britain since 1880*, Macmillan Press, London, 2000, Michael Schofield *The Sexual Behaviour of Young Adults*, Allen Lane, London, 1973; **p.80** Germaine Greer, *The Female Eunuch* (MacGibbon & Kee, 1970), copyright © Germaine Greer, 1970, 1971; **p.81** Violet Winspear quoted on http://www.goodreads.com/author/show/5029.Violet_Winspear, Maggie Alderson quote from http://maggiealderson.blogspot.co.uk/2010/03/female-eunuch-by-germaine-greer.html; **p.104** Hugh Greene quoted on http://www.bbc.co.uk/comedy/twtwtw/.
Permission for re-use of all © Crown copyright information is granted under the terms of the Open Government Licence (OGL).

Every effort has been made to trace all copyright holders, but if any have been inadvertently overlooked, the Publishers will be pleased to make the necessary arrangements at the first opportunity.

The Schools History Project

Set up in 1972 to bring new life to history for students aged 13–16, the Schools History Project continues to play an innovatory role in secondary history education. From the start, SHP aimed to show how good history has an important contribution to make to the education of a young person. It does this by creating courses and materials which both respect the importance of up-to-date, well-researched history and provide enjoyable learning experiences for students.

Since 1978 the Project has been based at Trinity and All Saints University College Leeds. It continues to support, inspire and challenge teachers through the annual conference, regional courses and website: http://www.schoolshistoryproject.org.uk. The Project is also closely involved with government bodies and awarding bodies in the planning of courses for Key Stage 3, GCSE and A level.

For teacher support material for this title, visit www.schoolshistoryproject.org.uk.

Although every effort has been made to ensure that website addresses are correct at time of going to press, Hodder Education cannot be held responsible for the content of any website mentioned in this book. It is sometimes possible to find a relocated web page by typing in the address of the home page for a website in the URL window of your browser.

Hachette UK's policy is to use papers that are natural, renewable and recyclable products and made from wood grown in sustainable forests. The logging and manufacturing processes are expected to conform to the environmental regulations of the country of origin.

Orders: please contact Bookpoint Ltd, 130 Milton Park, Abingdon, Oxon OX14 4SB. Telephone: +44 (0)1235 827720. Fax: +44 (0)1235 400454. Lines are open 9.00a.m.–5.00p.m., Monday to Saturday, with a 24-hour message answering service. Visit our website at www.hoddereducation.co.uk.

© Diana Laffin 2013

First published in 2013 by
Hodder Education,
an Hachette UK company
London NW1 3BH

Impression number	10 9 8 7 6 5 4 3 2 1
Year	2017 2016 2015 2014 2013

All rights reserved. Apart from any use permitted under UK copyright law, no part of this publication may be reproduced or transmitted in any form or by any means, electronic or mechanical, including photocopying and recording, or held within any information storage and retrieval system, without permission in writing from the publisher or under licence from the Copyright Licensing Agency Limited. Further details of such licences (for reprographic reproduction) may be obtained from the Copyright Licensing Agency Limited, Saffron House, 6–10 Kirby Street, London EC1N 8TS.

Typeset in 10pt Usherwood Book
Designed by Lorraine Inglis Design
Artwork by Oxford Designers and Illustrators, Lorraine Inglis Design and Barking Dog
Printed and bound in Italy
A catalogue record for this title is available from the British Library
ISBN 978 1 4441 4452 9

Contents

WAKEFIELD LIBRARIES & INFO. SERVICES	
30000010269388	
Bertrams	11/06/2013
941.085	£11.99

1 Introduction: The story of modern Britain

I was born in 1959, a child of the 1960s and 1970s, which puts me in the middle of this book. This has advantages.

The Second World War was still a haunting presence in my childhood. My dad wore his army shorts on holidays and my first home had an air raid shelter in the basement and hen houses in the garden. My granny was fanatical about not wasting food and we ate **spam** sandwiches on picnics. When I look at photos of families and their homes in the 1940s and 1950s, I recognise some of the clothes and furnishings of my own early childhood.

My children were born in the 1980s. They can hardly remember a world without the internet and satellite television. They have grown up in a Britain that is technically advanced, sexually liberated and ethnically diverse. Naturally they challenge my values and assumptions; they laugh at my incompetence with mobile phones and my discomfort with some of the more sexually explicit television series.

So in some ways I am well placed to review the past 60 years as my family experiences can help me to look back on the war-battered Britain of the 1940s and to examine the diverse and modern Britain of the twenty-first century. My family is in no way a 'typical' British family, if such a thing could exist. But placing them in the timeline of our evolving, modern nation is a useful reminder that this book is about people and how their lives have changed. That's important because social history is quite

spam
Canned pork meat, which was very popular in the war years

▷ The author's family in 1959.

2

different from the political history you may have studied before. The French Revolution or the reign of Charles I are well-defined topics, like rivers, with beginnings and ends and a strong historical current running through them. The 60 years of social history touched on in this book are more like an ocean: a mass of competing and ill-defined currents. It's easy to get lost in such a huge and complex topic and this book only touches on a few corners of this vast sea. The story of my family and other stories of individual people help to make intangible issues, such as changes in sexual attitudes, more comprehensible. But, even with this aid, you'll notice that few enquiries end with strong, clear judgements. With such complicated and wide-ranging issues, you need to treat generalisations with suspicion and recognise that caution is a virtue.

◁ The author's family in 2012.

My family has expanded over the last 50 years. I'm the baby in the first picture (opposite) taken in 1959. The second picture (above) shows us all celebrating my brother's 60th birthday in 2012. My mother is now the grandmother of eighteen grandchildren and great grandmother of two. The changes over the intervening years have been immense: technological, social, political and economic. In this book you will examine some of the extraordinary changes that have occurred in Britain in the last 60 years.

And yet, as these two pictures suggest, some aspects of Britain have remained remarkably constant. For most British people family relationships remain central to their lives. Look in a man's wallet or a woman's handbag, on desks at work, on computer screensavers, bedside tables or on Facebook and, more often than not, you'll find a family photo. The British are still ruled by a queen; they love fishing and gardening; they drink too much and they have unrealistic expectations of their sports stars.

Not everything has changed!

Through the decades: 1940s

Britain celebrates VE day and the end of the war. Britain has suffered extensive war damage and rationing continues. Labour wins a landslide election victory in 1945 and introduces a range of welfare reforms including the National Health Service (NHS). Major industries such as coal mining are taken over by the state. There are serious housing shortages.

1940

1945

My mum is in the crowds in London on VE day and cycles back to her home village in Surrey to see her young brother perched on the bus shelter attaching bunting across the street. My dad is 'demobbed' as a medical officer from the RAF. His letters show that he is a bit worried about how the plans for the new NHS will affect his independence as a doctor but nevertheless both my parents start long careers in the new service.

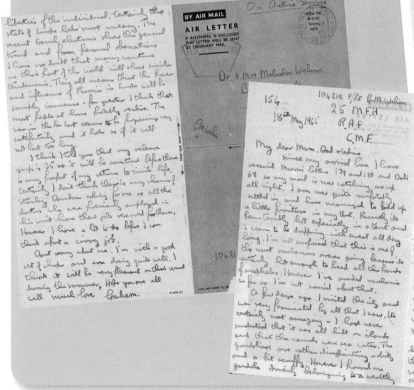

Through the decades: 1950s

Rationing disappears and the economy begins to prosper. The Queen's coronation is broadcast on television. According to Prime Minister Harold Macmillan, 'Most of our people have never had it so good'. By 1959 one in three UK families owns a car and most have a fridge in the kitchen. Commonwealth immigration rises and there are clashes between new immigrants and **Teddy boys**.

Teddy boys
Young, mostly working-class men, who wore Edwardian-style clothes and often prowled the streets in gangs

1950   1955

My mum and dad marry, buy their first house in Sheffield and have lots of children (they are bucking the trend – the UK birth rate is falling!). My mum buys her own little car to help her with her part-time medical work.

Through the decades: 1960s

Britain becomes more 'permissive' – divorce is made easier and homosexuality and abortion are legalised for the first time. There is a big growth in television sales and young people are swept up in the new popular music, films and fashions. The Labour leader, Harold Wilson, makes a speech about the 'white heat' of the technological and scientific revolution affecting Britain. Tensions rise over the issue of immigration with immigration controls and Enoch Powell's so-called 'Rivers of Blood' speech. There's great excitement when England win the World Cup in 1966.

1960

1965

I scream alongside my sisters when The Beatles appear on *Top of the Pops* and hide behind the settee when *Dr Who* is shown on our small black and white television. My sister sees the film *The Sound of Music* at the cinema eleven times. My mum helps to open a family planning clinic which actually gives advice to unmarried women.

Through the decades: 1970s

Tensions between the Government, employers and the unions trouble the decade, leading to the 'three-day week' and the 'Winter of Discontent'. Women demand better rights and finally win equal pay. Most families now have a television and washing machine. Britain joins the EEC and the coinage is decimalised. It is the years of Punk and Glam Rock. Royalty is still respected – the Queen's Silver Jubilee is widely celebrated. Margaret Thatcher comes to power in 1979.

1970

1975

My mum, horrified by the lives of poor women in Glasgow (where we moved to in 1967), writes an article for the paper about battered wives. Our first dishwasher and freezer arrive in the home. We all have a day off school for Princess Anne's wedding. I go off to university. My boyfriend falls into drunken despair when Margaret Thatcher wins the election in 1979 and passes out on my bed.

Through the decades: 1980s

yuppies
Young upwardly mobile professionals. In the 1980s there were growing numbers of well-qualified young people who made a lot of money and enjoyed an affluent lifestyle

Mrs Thatcher introduces public spending cuts, privatises major industries and challenges the power of the trade unions. Unemployment rises. The Miners' Strike leads to violent clashes with the police. Race riots occur in several different cities. The IRA remains active and deaths from terrorist incidents reach a peak. Four leading Labour politicians found a new political party, the Social Democrats (SDP). Personal computers and microwave ovens make an impact and it is the age of **yuppies** and, for many, higher standards of living.

1980

1985

I graduate but there are no jobs! I go to work in Brixton Unemployment Office a few months after the riots, walking with a rape alarm in my pocket, just in case. After finishing my teacher training, I get a job in a school in Berkshire and go on strike for the first time. My mum votes for Roy Jenkins, one of the SDP's 'Gang of Four', in the Hillhead by-election and he wins the seat. My older two children are born in the local hospital but the maternity unit is closed by the time my youngest is born: one of the many 1980s cuts.

Through the decades: 1990s–2000s

The personal computer, the mobile phone and the internet become everyday aspects of people's lives while satellite television and video recorders transform the nation's viewing habits. Attitudes to royalty are changed by two royal divorces and the death of Diana, Princess of Wales. Tony Blair sweeps the Labour Party to power with a landslide victory in 1997, bringing an end to eighteen years of Conservative rule.

Labour remains in power and involves Britain in wars in Afghanistan and Iraq. Muslim extremism becomes a serious issue, especially after bomb attacks in London. Both Scotland and Wales get devolved Parliaments. Laws on discrimination are tightened up and civil partnerships for same-sex couples are introduced. The 'credit crunch' heralds an economic depression from 2007 onwards.

1990   2000   2010

We buy a family computer and send our first e-mails. At my school we get our first 'computer suite' and I am trained in how to use the internet for lessons. Princess Diana's death shocks us and I queue at the local town hall to sign the book of condolence.

The lives of my nieces reflect many of the social changes in Britain. One marries an immigrant from Sierra Leone, another has a baby before she marries and a third celebrates a civil partnership. These are all causes of celebration, not consternation, in my family. As my college is in the middle of a military area, I am very aware that friends and relatives of those I work with are risking their lives abroad. My children grow up and leave home but in the recession finding jobs proves difficult.

How far has Britain changed?

Although Britain never faced Nazi occupation, it emerged from the Second World War a battered and exhausted nation. It was a land of rules, queues and shortages. Yet the 1945 election confirmed that wartime patriotism was going to be no barrier to social change. The Labour government which swept to a landslide victory instituted some of the most radical social and economic reforms of the twentieth century, with the new National Health Service one of its main achievements. The war had both exposed and challenged social inequality. Evacuation meant that children from London's East End had moved in with middle-class country families; officers and men had served together in the forces and rationing had established a sense of state-imposed fairness. Despite this, British society in 1945 was very different from Britain in the twenty-first century as the historian, David Kynaston, a specialist on this period, explains:

> Britain in 1945. A land of orderly queues, hat-doffing men walking on the outside, seats given up to the elderly, no swearing in front of the women and children, censored books, censored films, censored plays, infinite repression of desires. Divorce for most an unthinkable social disgrace, marriage too often a life sentence ... Even the happier marriages seldom companionable, with husbands and wives living in separate, self-contained spheres, the husband often not telling the wife how much he earned. And despite women working in wartime jobs, few quarrelling with the assumption that the two sexes were fundamentally different from each other. Children in the street ticked off by strangers, children in the street kept an eye on by strangers, children at home rarely consulted, children stopped being children when they left home at 14 and got a job. A land of hierarchical social assumptions, of accent and dress as giveaways to class, of Irish jokes and casually derogatory references to Jews and niggers.
>
> (D. Kynaston, *Austerity Britain 1945–48: A World to Build* (2007))

How much of the Britain of the 1940s has been lost in our twenty-first century nation? The writer A. N. Wilson strongly argues in his book on modern Britain that the country of his parents, 'my Britain', no longer exists:

> During the Second World War, and in the times of economic austerity thereafter we were – yes, it makes sense to use the first person plural – we were an entity. The young men, of whatever social class, did National Service together. Rich and poor had received identical rations, fairly shared. With the coming of prosperity – prosperity which almost everyone must surely have welcomed – the problems began. The inhabitants of the British archipelago became a collection of classes and races and individuals, living side by side and for the most part trying to ignore one another.
>
> (A. N. Wilson, *Our Times: The Age of Elizabeth II* (2008))

Few modern historians share Wilson's negative view of the last 60 years. Many point to the achievements of the period – rising living standards, growing toleration and celebration of multi-culturalism. A 2007 survey showed that two-thirds of British people considered 'Britishness' as important and that the British felt more patriotic about their country than almost any other European state.

This more positive view is confirmed by research in 2009 which ranked European countries on a series of measures and reached the following conclusions about Britain:

- Civil liberties are high in the UK, as is perceived tolerance for minorities and immigrants.
- The UK has a highly effective and transparent government with low levels of corruption.
- Nearly ten out of ten Britons felt that they have friends or family to rely on in times of need.

Modern politicians, such as former Prime Minister Gordon Brown, have claimed that key British values such as decency, toleration and fairness are enduring and consistent facets of the British nation. But this strong claim would certainly be challenged by many minority groups who have suffered years of discrimination. This disagreement is a powerful example of the problems in reaching judgements about social history. Do you judge social progress in comparison with other European states or by standards in the past? Do you use the 'hard' evidence of statistics or listen to the memories of grandparents? Clearly, there are different perspectives according to class, age, gender and ethnicity. Which one is right?

The challenge of the enquiries in this book is to accept that there won't be right answers. Of course there are some changes that can be identified with confidence: the legalisation of homosexuality and rising living standards are examples. But this book tackles much less concrete issues such as how far attitudes to women have changed and how far British values have been moulded by the media. Some judgements will be offered in response to these questions, but they will be *suggestions, not answers*.

A further dimension to the study of social history is the great mass of complex evidence at hand. Sources in social history come in all sorts of forms: statistics, diaries, newspapers and images. Each chapter of this book concludes with an Insight panel inviting you to take 'a closer look' at such material and consider how to use it carefully and critically.

My invitation to you as you reflect on the arguments and the evidence before you is to reach your own cautious judgements on the key question underlying each chapter in this book: how far has Britain changed since 1945?

When, if ever, did Britain become a multi-cultural society?

1950s	Fish and chips in newspaper
1960s	Chinese restaurants/ take-aways
1970s	Indian restaurants take off. Chicken Tikka Masala appeared first in the 1960s possibly in Glasgow, and Balti in the 1980s in Birmingham.
1980s	Asian ready meals
2000s	Reggae Reggae Sauce

> **Question:** What could be more British than fish and chips?
>
> **Answer:** Chicken Tikka Masala?

In 2001 the politician Robin Cook announced that this was the nation's favourite dish and an example of 'multi-culturalism as a positive force for our economy and our society'. In fact, neither dish is truly British or foreign. Fried fish probably derived from Jewish cooking traditions and chips are almost certainly French in origin, combining them only developing from the 1920s onwards. Chicken Tikka Masala is an Indian dish that you could not find in India. It was concocted by clever Asian restaurant chefs in Britain needing to provide cheap, quick food that was palatable for local taste. So both dishes are ingenious British creations made from 'foreign' ideas and ingredients. It is often said that 'You are what you eat', so what does the British diet tell us about our national identity?

In the past 50 years British food has been transformed by immigration. Mashed potato, cabbage and spam, the typical 'meat and two veg' meals of the post-war years, have been replaced by an astonishing array of new foods from across the world. In the 1950s, few British families would eat out and the only take-away option was fish and chips wrapped in newspaper. Now a typical British town has several Chinese take-aways, Indian restaurants, American fast food outlets or pizza suppliers. And there is no doubt that it has been immigrants who have been at the forefront of this culinary revolution. They introduced ready meals such as Vestas (just add water) in the 1960s, set up food supply companies such as Tilda rice, and ran innumerable small restaurant and take-away businesses. Cities in industrial decline such as Bradford were revitalised in the 1980s by the blossoming of curry houses. More recently Alan Yau, originally from Hong Kong, launched the Japanese noodle restaurants Wagamama in the 1990s and the Jamaican Levi Roots won national recognition for his spicy Reggae Reggae Sauce. Nowhere is Britain's multi-cultural diversity more evident than in our diet.

Some suggest that this is proof of the success of modern immigration into Britain. Our love affair with curry, our eagerness to try new tastes and our appreciation of the services on offer have broken down barriers and suspicions. But this may be over-optimistic. It is Bengali and Chinese food, in particular, which has made such an impact on the British diet; the large Afro-Caribbean community has not had a similar influence. And the Indian and Chinese food we eat, Ken Lo has pointed out, is a 'construct' – in other words a version of Asian food adjusted for Western customers that is quite different from the authentic food eaten by Indian or Chinese families at home.

> The Indian food eaten by the ethnic majority represents a multi-cultural compromise, a symbol of a superficial level of exchange between the majority and one particular minority.
>
> (P. Panayi, 'Immigration, multiculturalism and racism' in F. Carnevali and J. M. Strange (editors) *20th Century Britain: Economic, Cultural and Social Change* (second edition 2007)).

Eating in an Indian restaurant does not necessarily lead to racial harmony; incidences of white customers abusing Indian waiting staff are not uncommon. For some ethnic groups, such as Orthodox Jews, the strict rules of food supply and preparation can still be a source of isolation rather than integration. And the view that food businesses have resulted in uniform success and profits for the immigrant community is also inaccurate. Research suggests that for many small-scale operations the hours are long and the pay low. Although more than 85 per cent of curry restaurants are owned and run by Muslims, their popularity has coincided with years of growing **Islamophobia** and racist attacks on the Asian community.

So it is safe to conclude that Britain's food has been transformed by immigration. But is the story of our changing diet really one of progression to a genuinely multi-cultural society? Or is it a story of superficial and partial compromise that camouflages enduring divisions and inequalities? In the early twenty-first century the merits of a 'multi-cultural compromise' were being seriously challenged. With growing fears resulting from the 2001 terrorist attacks on New York, there was increasingly outspoken insistence, by the public and by politicians, that immigrants should adapt to British customs. Minority communities themselves questioned whether multi-cultural policies have protected them from persistent discrimination. Post-war Britain may have tasted multi-culturalism, but how far it has ever been truly absorbed in our hearts, minds (or even stomachs!) remains highly debatable.

Islamophobia
Hatred, fear or dislike of people of the Muslim faith

Charan Gill

It is difficult to imagine what a culture shock it must have been for Charan Gill, arriving in Glasgow in 1963, at the age of nine. Used to the warmth and colour of the Punjab, he now faced the rain and darkness of Scottish winters in a city of tall tenements and coal fires. His father had worked long hours on the buses to save up the money to buy a small flat before sending for his wife and children to join him. But his son turned down the opportunities of a British further education and left school aged sixteen to work in the shipyards.

It was a tough environment for an Indian Sikh but he enjoyed his apprenticeship and might have stayed on as a shipbuilder if he hadn't happened to see an old friend when walking down a city street one evening. Gurmail Dhillon, who was running the Ashoka Indian restaurant, was looking exhausted and Charan offered to help out. He started by cleaning toilets and peeling onions after his shipyard shifts, but then decided, in 1984, to go into partnership with his friend.

Like other Indian restaurants at that time, they exploited the demand for take-away

△ Charan Gill.

meals and adapted their menus to local tastes. Borrowing money from friends and using his savings, Charan expanded his empire so that by the twenty-first century he was known in Glasgow as the 'Curry King', had seventeen restaurants and an MBE. Immensely proud of both his Indian and his Scottish heritage, he has even invented a new garment, a 'tartan shehrvani', combining Scottish and Indian clothing traditions.

Britain's mixed society

In 1945, Britain was a mixed but overwhelmingly white society. Most of the immigrant communities up to that point had come from Europe, with the biggest groups being Irish or European Jews fleeing persecution. After the war, many Poles and Italians settled in Britain and there were approximately 20,000 Asian or black workers, many employed in the docks, on merchant ships or in the armed services.

In 2001 the census showed that Britain was still more than 90 per cent white, although the proportion of people with Asian, African or Afro-Caribbean descent had grown rapidly with post-war immigration, particularly in urban areas. Another important feature was the growing number of people with mixed backgrounds; a reminder that labelling people by their race can be problematic. Britain has one of the fastest growing mixed-race populations in the world.

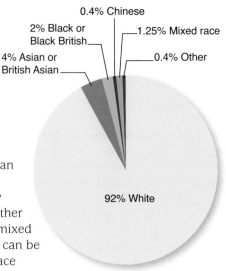

△ Ethnic diversity in England and Wales in 2001.
Source: Census 2001.

Changing ideas about Britain's mixed society

Britain has always been a multi-cultural society, in the sense that people of different colours, faiths, nations and cultures have lived together here. The years since 1945 have seen much larger waves of immigration, particularly from Asia and the Caribbean, simultaneous with the loss of empire. This has led to intense discussion about how immigrants interact with British society, with different ideas evolving over time:

1   **Assimilation:** Up until the mid-1960s immigrants were expected to fit in with British society as quickly as they could. The underlying assumption was that British culture was superior and that all immigrants should want to adopt the British way of life.

2   **Integration:** In 1966 the liberal Home Secretary Roy Jenkins called for integration, defining this as 'not a flattening process of uniformity, but cultural diversity, coupled with equality of opportunity in an atmosphere of mutual tolerance'.

3   **Multi-culturalism:** From the 1970s there was a movement to go beyond tolerance and acceptance of different faiths and cultures towards a positive celebration of diversity. Schools, local authorities and arts organisations promoted this policy.

4   **Community cohesion:** In the twenty-first century concern has risen about the disaffection of minority communities and the need to bind British society together by emphasising shared values of tolerance and respect.

■ Enquiry Focus: When, if ever, did Britain become a multi-cultural society?

The focus of this enquiry is the term 'multi-cultural' – so we need to define it. It means more than just the existence of a variety of ethnic traditions, languages, arts and faiths within one community. It has been defined in contrasting ways, depending often on whether or not the writer supports it and we will be returning to the problem of definition at the end. But for the purpose of this enquiry, we will use four measures of the extent of multi-culturalism: how far have first- and second-generation migrants to Britain:

1 achieved **economic well-being** in the UK (£)

2 contributed to the development of British **culture**, including food, music and the arts (C)

3 won equal **political recognition** and rights, in the workplace and in British institutions (R)

4 become **socially integrated** – mixing with and being accepted by the communities in which they settle (S)?

A useful way to record your conclusions is to create a timeline like the one below. As you work your way through the chapter, make notes on the timeline to cover each measure.

Remember that there will be many 'grey areas'. Don't be tempted to jump to conclusions or make definite judgements. To help you with this problem, the first two measures are considered on the next two spreads with some guidance on the kinds of conclusions you could reach. The key points are also added to the timeline.

As you work through the rest of the chapter, add further notes to cover points 3 and 4 using the codes (R) and (S). This will give you a useful basis for your final review at the end of the chapter.

☐ Fully multi-cultural

☐ Not at all multi-cultural

C Diverse religious festivals and places of worship are accepted as part of British life.

£ Second-generation immigrants prospered compared to new migrants.

£ Asian community had high rates of self-employment and home ownership.

C New food outlets such as Chinese take-aways and Indian restaurants become an established part of British towns.

£ Ugandan Asians settled and prospered very quickly.

C Caribbean music such as reggae is enjoyed by a wide section of the British public.

£ Report showed that most immigrants were doing better than UK-born population (2005).

| 1950s | 1960s | 1970s | 1980s | 1990s | 2000s |

£ Immigrants arriving from the Caribbean, India and Pakistan earned low wages and had menial jobs.

£ Some immigrant groups such as the Bangladeshi community suffered persistent poverty.

C By the 1980s black sportsmen and women are valued on the football field and the running track.

£ In recessions in the 1980s and 1990s ethnic minorities had higher rates of unemployment than white workers.

C Cultural acceptance is patchy – little representation of ethnic minorities in theatre and film.

£ Immigrants had lower average wages than other British workers in the 1980s and early 1990s. They were under-represented in high status jobs.

Measure 1: Have immigrants to Britain achieved economic well-being?

Yes, they have

Immigrants are people who have arrived in a new country, **emigrants** are people who have left their own country and **migrants** are people who moved from one place to another.

■ A report for the Institute of Public Policy Research in 2005 concluded that 'on most criteria, most immigrant groups do better in economic terms than the UK-born population'.

■ Although first-generation migrants suffered lower incomes, this disadvantage diminished the longer they lived in the UK and was greatly reduced in the second generation.

■ Many immigrants have successfully set up their own businesses and shown a flair for entrepreneurship. In 2005 around 13 per cent of those born within the UK were self-employed, compared to 33 per cent of those born in Pakistan. Ugandan Asians, arriving in the UK in the 1970s, were quick to prosper and by 2000 had businesses employing more than 30,000 people. It is likely, however, that many immigrants set up their own businesses because they faced discrimination in the job market.

■ Asians, in particular, have had higher than average levels of home ownership. More than a third of those born in India or Pakistan owned their own homes in 2005 compared to 27 per cent of those born in the UK.

▷ The independence and prosperity of Britain's immigrant community is clear on urban high streets throughout the UK.

No, they haven't

■ Members of ethnic minorities tended to work in low-paid and menial jobs. In the 1950s and 1960s immigrants were recruited to help Britain's shortage of workers in less popular jobs in transport and hospitals. The 1991 census showed that two-thirds of those of Caribbean, Pakistani and Bangladeshi background worked in manual jobs compared to only 50 per cent for whites. Ethnic minorities have been consistently under-represented in high status jobs, for instance, they represented less than 1 per cent of judges at this time.

- Migrants to Britain generally have been paid lower wages than would be expected from their qualifications and experience. West Indians with ten years' experience would, on average, earn 28 per cent less than their white equivalents in the post-war years. Indian and Pakistani workers also earned lower wages in the 1960s and 1970s. Even in the years 1985–95 the average salary of Pakistani and Bangladeshi men was just over half that of whites and the wages of Caribbean and African men was around two-thirds of the pay of white workers.

- The black and Asian communities have suffered much higher levels of unemployment in periods of recession. In the period 1984–92 research showed that black men experienced 30 per cent higher job losses than white men and in 1997–98 joblessness among the black and Pakistani communities was more than twice the level of whites.

- Some ethnic minorities have been much less prosperous than others. The Bangladeshi community has suffered longer term poverty than most other immigrant groups, with more than 60 per cent of those arriving from Bangladesh earning less than half the British median wage in the early twenty-first century, and only 13 per cent owning their own homes in 2005 (compared to 27 per cent of white households).

■ The historical problem: the qualified conclusion

So what is the answer to the question: 'Have immigrants to Britain achieved economic well-being?' As you can see from the timeline, the evidence is contradictory and complex. There are numerous factors that have influenced living standards and employment over the last 50 years. Immigrant families, for instance, are far more likely to live in cities, especially London, where wages are generally higher. There is also a big difference between those who were born abroad and those who were brought up in the UK; the longer someone has lived in the UK, the closer their earnings are likely to be to British norms. Additionally, there are variations between ethnic minority groups arising from their cultural and educational backgrounds and the resources they arrive with.

Good historians are usually cautious of simple conclusions because historical questions, like the one above, rarely have simple answers. Qualifying your conclusion – that is, recognising the 'ifs and buts' – is not the same as sitting on the fence. Strong conclusions to essays often make more than one judgement rather than trying to say it all in one sentence. In the case of economic well-being, we might write:

'Once immigrants have been settled in the UK for some time, most have achieved a reasonable standard of living, many of them setting up businesses and owning their own homes. On arrival in Britain, however, many faced discrimination in the job market, and some immigrant communities have continued to live in deprived neighbourhoods with lower average wages and higher unemployment rates than those born in the UK.'

Measure 2: Have immigrants contributed to the development of British culture, including food, music and the arts?

Unlike the last question the answer to this one seems simple and obvious – of course they have. We have already looked at how British food has been revolutionised by immigration. Music is another field that has been hugely enriched, especially by the Afro-Caribbean community. A rich variety of festivals are now enjoyed throughout the year and cities are brightened by Chinatowns, mosques and gurdwaras.

Yet, even in the area of culture, it is dangerous to make generalisations. A much more open attitude to ethnic diversity has only really developed since the 1980s. Certain aspects of particular cultures and traditions have been appreciated by the British majority but others have not. Chinese take-aways and reggae music were quickly popularised but Bollywood films and Afro-Caribbean food were not part of mainstream culture until much more recently. Until the 1990s, ethnic minorities remained greatly under-represented in film, television and theatre. Furthermore, it is possible that strong associations of one branch of art and culture with particular ethnic groups can re-enforce cultural stereotyping. A report of 2008 showed that many teachers had, sometimes unconsciously, made assumptions such as that black children are good at sport, the Chinese talented at maths and cooking and the Indians efficient at running businesses. This was limiting rather than improving the opportunities of ethnic minority children in schools.

△ The Guru Nanak Gurdwara in Smethwick, Birmingham. Originally the site of a church, this gurdwara has hosted annual Shaheedi Tournaments since 1963. These games are held in the memory of current and past martyrs of the Sikh religion.

△ The Chinese Archway in Liverpool is the largest in the western world. It stands across the entrance to the city's Chinatown, full of Chinese restaurants and businesses. Apart from the arch itself, erected in 2000, within this area there are Chinese-style lampposts, litter boxes and even parking ticket machines. The area is the centre of the Chinese New Year festivities.

Three British Jamaican sporting stars

- **Viv Anderson**, the son of Jamaican immigrants, was the first black footballer to be capped for England in 1978.
- **Errol Christie**'s parents arrived in England from Jamaica in the 1950s and he went on to become the European boxing champion and leader of the British boxing team in the early 1980s.
- **Tessa Sanderson** was born in Jamaica, coming over to England aged six. She won the Olympic Gold medal for the javelin in 1984.

All three overcame violent prejudice and poor backgrounds to achieve success. Anderson was pelted with bananas when playing for Nottingham Forest in the 1970s. Christie had to fight racist gangs when walking in his home city Coventry and Sanderson was spat at and called a golliwog at school. Yet they provided excellent role models for other aspiring sportsmen and women, especially those with Caribbean backgrounds.

■ The historical problem: typicality

What do the stories of these three Jamaicans tell us? Their lives are certainly not typical. Most Jamaicans, even those of the second generation, did not find fame and fortune through sport. More likely they stayed in the communities they grew up in and earned below average wages in factories, buses or hospitals. They enjoyed their own music, food and traditions within their own neighbourhoods but not beyond them. They faced discrimination, which often limited their opportunities. There were lots of Jamaicans who had no sporting talent at all.

Yet these three were not the exceptions that proved the rule either. Sport and music were important routes out of poverty for those with talent, determination and a bit of luck. The examples set by Anderson, Christie and Sanderson affected attitudes within and outside the Jamaican community, challenging the negative stereotypes of '**yardies**' that were common at this time. They blazed a trail that many others have followed. So their careers were significant, if not typical.

It is an essential job of an historian to make judgements about the past while avoiding sweeping generalisations. Individual stories throw light on personal experience and this is vital if we are to truly understand what went on. These stories then need to be compared and contrasted with others and put in the context of more general trends before any firm judgements can be made. So, in the case of cultural contributions we might write:

'Immigrants have made an enormous contribution to British culture in the last 60 years. There has been a growing appreciation of ethnic food and music and an acceptance of diverse religions and traditions. In certain fields, such as sport, black participation has become highly valued. Nevertheless, cultural achievement and recognition have been uneven in pace and extent, with some areas such as theatre and film remaining white-dominated until very recently.'

yardies
Slang term for Jamaicans involved in gang culture; often associated with guns and illegal drugs

■ Your enquiry from now on

For the remainder of the chapter, add relevant points to your timeline showing progress or lack of progress towards social integration and political recognition for the immigrant community. Use the first two topics on economic well-being and contribution to culture as models to follow.

When, if ever, did the British government adopt multi-culturalism?

Many factors influenced the British government's immigration policies in the post-war years, including the desire to keep the Commonwealth together and to improve economic efficiency. There's no doubt, however, that government policy was dominated by fear and guilt. *Fear* of the rising numbers of ethnic minority immigrants led to a series of immigration controls that have been based more on race than reason. *Guilt* at the discrimination faced by new arrivals led to race relations measures that attempted to safeguard the rights of those minorities once they had settled here. The assumption governing these policies since the mid-1960s was summed up by Roy Hattersley: 'without integration limitation is inexcusable; without limitation integration is impossible'. Too many people with alien cultures, faiths and skins would surely undermine the British way of life. But the British way of life included a respect for equal rights under the law once the immigrants had arrived. This uneasy mix of prejudice and acceptance is summarised in the diagram on this spread. At what time, if any, did the British government truly embrace multi-culturalism?

> ■ Pick out the key changes in the laws that affected social integration and political rights to add to your timeline diagram.

FEAR Immigration Controls	KEY DEVELOPMENTS	GUILT Race Relations Policies
	During the Second World War colonial troops, refugees and European freedom fighters had all been based in Britain. The Soviet occupation of Eastern Europe and Britain's growing labour shortage meant that many stayed.	
1947 Polish Resettlement Act enabled 200,000 Polish war veterans to settle in the UK.		
1948: The British Nationality Act gave all Commonwealth subjects British citizenship, recognising their right to work and settle in the UK and to bring their families with them.	In 1948 the *SS Empire Windrush* docked with just under 500 Caribbean men in June 1948. There followed a rise in numbers, reaching a peak of more than 66,000 in 1961. South Asian immigration also reached a peak in the early 1960s.	A **Royal Commission on Population** reported in **1949** that immigrants to Britain should be 'of good human stock' and able and willing to inter-marry with the resident population.
	Riots broke out in Nottingham and Notting Hill in 1958 between right-wing groups, Teddy boys and newly settled immigrants.	In **1965** the first **Race Relations Act** made it illegal to discriminate against people on the grounds of their race, nationality or ethnicity in public places. It did not cover either housing or employment where there was widespread prejudice against immigrants. In 1967 the Joint Council for the Welfare of Immigrants was set up.

1962 Commonwealth Immigrants Act restricted access to the UK, making it dependent on employment vouchers which gave preference to those with employment already organised in the UK or with skills and qualifications needed. This excluded the majority of possible immigrants from the West Indies and Asia. In 1965 the number of vouchers was reduced to 8500 a year. This Act was followed by further restrictions in 1968.

1971 Immigration Act restricted entry to the UK to those who had a specific job for a specific period. Entry of family members was further restricted and police and immigration officials were given wide-ranging powers.

The British Nationality Act of 1981 introduced new definitions of British citizenship making a clear distinction between those with 'a close connection' to the UK and those without. The right to reside in Britain was restricted to the first category.

Acts passed in **1986** and **1988** further restricted immigration.

British Nationality (Hong Kong) Act 1990 limited numbers allowed into the UK.

In **2001** new security measures were passed in Parliament.

In 1968 Kenyan Asians left Africa following discrimination against them. In 1972, 60,000 Asians were forced to leave Uganda by Idi Amin. The rules of the newly restrictive Immigration Act of 1971 were bent in order to let 27,000 into the UK.

In the 1970s Greek Cypriots and Vietnamese refugees arrived in Britain following political unrest in their own countries.

In 1981, riots caused by racial tensions and urban poverty erupted in Leeds, Liverpool, the West Midlands and Brixton in London. There were further riots in Birmingham and London in 1985.

The inadequate London police investigation into the murder of Stephen Lawrence, a black teenager stabbed to death at a bus stop, led to a major enquiry.

Hong Kong was formally handed over to Chinese rule in 1997 preceded by a rise in emigration from the area.

The terrorist attack on New York's Twin Towers in 2001 led to new fears about Islamic extremism.

Growing numbers of asylum seekers arrived in the UK. As new Eastern European countries joined the EU, immigration to the UK reached a new peak.

1968 Race Relations Act broadened the scope of the 1965 Act to make racial discrimination in housing or employment illegal.

1976 Race Relations Act strengthened the law against discrimination by covering all employees and using a broader definition of discrimination. It also set up the **Commission for Racial Equality** with the aims of promoting racial equality and fighting injustice.

The Scarman Report (1981) on the Brixton riots stressed the 'racial disadvantage that is a fact of British life'. Recommendations for better community policing and tackling black poverty were made.

The Macpherson Report (1999) into the death of Stephen Lawrence accused the police of 'institutional racism' leading to a number of new measures including the **Race Relations Act of 2000** which obliged public bodies to fight against racism.

Laws in **2003** and **2006** made religious discrimination in employment and inciting religious hatred into crimes.

△ 1958: An immigrant
reading a sign on a
boarding house door,
which says 'No
coloured men'.

ex-servicemen
Men who had served in
the armed forces in the war

What does this
suggest about
social integration?

The West Indian experience

'We won't have niggers in this hotel.' That was the response that greeted Learie
Constantine when he checked into the Imperial Hotel in London in 1943. A
renowned West Indian sportsman coming to London to run fund-raising cricket
matches for the Ministry of Labour, Constantine had been booked to stay for
four nights. When the manageress insisted he could only stay one, he moved to
the nearby Bedford Hotel where he was well treated. But the story didn't end
there. Constantine took the hotel to the High Court and employed a top
barrister to represent him. Racism was not illegal at this time so the case was
based on breach of contract. He won the case and was awarded damages. The
judge ruled that the language used had been 'deeply offensive' and Constantine
received hundreds of letters of congratulation from across the country.

This case highlights the mixed reception that awaited West Indian
immigrants to Britain in the post-war years. Their contribution to the war was
appreciated; more than 10,000 West Indians had volunteered to fight and a
further 15,000 had helped keep the supply routes open by working as
merchant seamen. They were also valued as employees in the growing
transport and health sectors. On the other hand, there was widespread and
enduring prejudice, suspicion and ignorance. Even before the arrival of the
SS Empire Windrush with nearly 500 Caribbean immigrants on board, there
had been a steady trickle of arrivals and by 1961 there were an estimated
100,000 Caribbean people living in London. The majority of the new arrivals
were young men, many **ex-servicemen**, and mostly with trades and skills to
offer. High unemployment, a slump in the sugar industry and severe hurricanes
in Jamaica combined with optimistic views of prospects awaiting them in
Britain, encouraged them to come. But many were deeply disappointed.

West Indian immigrants struggled to find decent accommodation in a
country still recovering from wartime bombing. Many landlords refused to let
property to black applicants; a survey in Birmingham in the 1950s revealed
that only 15 out of 1000 would do so. Immigrants congregated in poor areas,
were exploited by landlords and suffered from overcrowding and high rents.
Although most West Indians found jobs fairly rapidly, more than half had to
accept posts that were below the level of their skills and qualifications. In the
streets they often faced abuse and sometimes even violence, and were denied
entry to pubs and dance halls.

Racial tensions increased, especially in urban areas such as North London.
Right-wing groups, like the Union of British Freedom, targeted the newcomers,
distributing leaflets opposing 'the immigration of thousands of completely
different people who take our homes and threaten our jobs'. Walls were daubed
with slogans such as 'Keep Britain White'. Teddy boys would taunt black people
in the street and find reasons to pick a fight. In response, immigrants began to
defend themselves and some carried knives. Tensions rose to a peak in the late
summer of 1958 with serious riots in Nottingham and Notting Hill in London.
In London the riots were triggered by a group of youths going 'nigger hunting'
and followed by attacks on black people's homes, cafes and shops. The police
were slow to intervene and the violence continued for two weeks. When the
judge sent four white youths to prison for their part in the riots, he commented
that 'Everyone, irrespective of the colour of their skin, is entitled to walk
through our streets in peace, with their heads erect and free from fear.'

Despite this claim, the stabbing of a carpenter from Antigua, just a few months later, showed this was not the reality for many West Indians. Their response was a growing assertiveness and independence, especially shown in the celebration of Caribbean culture and music.

■ What does this suggest about political recognition?

> Before the riots I was British – I was born under the Union Jack, but the race riots made me realise who I am and what I am. They turned me into a staunch Jamaican. To think any other way would not have been kidding anyone else more than myself.
>
> (Baron Baker, a young West Indian commenting after the 1950s riots)

In the twenty years after the end of the war, immigrants struggled to be socially accepted and to win equal political rights. While the courts appeared to recognise their equality before the law, on the streets they faced prejudice, violence and intimidation. West Indians relied on their own mutually supportive communities and celebrated their culture within their own neighbourhoods. From the late 1960s culture was the means of breaking down barriers, for instance, reggae music and the Notting Hill Carnival began to be admired by the white community.

Caribbean music

One *Windrush* passenger was Aldwyn 'Lord Kitchener' Roberts, a calypso singer from Trinidad. He soon gained regular work in Brixton bars and pubs, helping to establish a strong Caribbean musical scene. Calypso gained a wider audience when Cy Grant appeared in the television show *Tonight* from 1957 to 1960, summarising news stories in a calypso song.

In the 1960s and 1970s, Caribbean music was strongly influenced by the **Black Power** and **Rastafarian movements**. Young black Britons identified with the emerging reggae music which often had political lyrics. Black teenagers with Rasta dreadlocks and hats, using their own slang and playing reggae music, challenged white authority in the streets and in the schools. While reggae flourished in West Indian clubs, it was not played on Radio 1 as there was thought to be little 'national demand' for it. A breakthrough came with Bob Marley and the Wailers' 1975 tour of Britain, which brought in fans of all colours and backgrounds. Reggae went on to develop new forms which were appreciated by a wide audience.

Black Power movement
This was the struggle for black civil rights which emerged in the USA in the late 1960s

Rastafarian movement
This started as a religious movement in Jamaica. Rastas reject Western culture and society and celebrate African ways of life

Claudia Jones and the Notting Hill Carnival
Buried next to Karl Marx in Highgate Cemetery in North London is a remarkable political activist from Trinidad. Claudia Jones was expelled from the USA for her Communist views in 1958 and immediately joined in the struggle for immigrants' rights in Britain. She launched the *West Indian Gazette*, the first British newspaper for black readers, and organised a Caribbean cultural evening in a hall in North London in January 1959 to help those caught up in the riots. Under the slogan 'A people's art is the genesis of their freedom', further concerts were held, later developing into the Notting Hill Carnival, a colourful celebration of Caribbean culture which now brightens up North London every August.

■ These cultural developments had significant social impact. In the shorter term they set the Caribbean community apart but later on became a means of better social acceptance. Note this down on your timeline.

How far did Britain become a multi-cultural society in the 1960s and 1970s? The Asian experience

■ Jolly's case is mainly about employment rights. Equal rights at work is about social acceptance as well as political recognition. You might like to note this on your timeline as a development that covers both.

△ Sikh police officers were officially given permission to wear a turban instead of the usual cap or helmet in 1969. Special Constable Harbans Singh Jabbal was the first British policeman to wear a turban on duty, at East Ham police station, January 1970.

Sohan Singh Jolly

In 1969, Sohan Singh Jolly, a former police inspector and war veteran from Wolverhampton, declared that he would commit suicide on Sunday 13 April by setting himself on fire. Mr Jolly was a respected local leader who described himself as 'moderate'. Yet he was determined to carry out his threat, won the support of his community at home and abroad and even the pledge of fourteen others to join in his suicide pact. Why?

Wearing a turban and a beard are important aspects of the Sikh faith. In August 1967 a bus driver in Wolverhampton had been sent home from work for wearing a turban. This led to a determined campaign by Mr Jolly and the Sikh community to have him re-instated and the right to wear turbans at work formally recognised.

The local transport committee held firm. Five thousand Sikhs marched through Wolverhampton in protest. The Indian High Commissioner and two government ministers appealed for a reversal of the rule. But the Mayor of Wolverhampton supported the turban ban and most of the white community agreed, one letter stating that Sikhs should remember that they were living in England, not India.

In the end, though, Mr Jolly won. The council announced on 9 April 1969 that 'in the interests of race relations' they had taken the decision to relax the rule. From that point on Sikhs were able to wear turbans and beards while at work.

Acceptance of different cultural traditions is a pre-requisite for successful social integration. It has often been the Asian community, with well-established customs of dress and behaviour, that has struggled to win that acceptance. Indian Sikhs were one group of South Asian immigrants to arrive in large numbers in the 1950s and 1960s. They came for better prospects and jobs and to escape the political and religious turmoil that followed the independence of India in 1947. Most Asians came from three main regions: Gujarat and Punjab in India, Mirpur in Pakistan, and Sylhet in Bangladesh, and they settled in London, the Midlands and larger northern cities such as Bradford and Glasgow. They had different religious faiths; many Indians were Hindus or Sikhs while a majority of Pakistani and Bangladeshi migrants were Muslim. Shared language, religion and culture bound these groups together in close-knit communities, around their places of worship in affordable inner city areas. It was unsurprising that social integration proved difficult, especially for these first-generation migrants.

Some barriers to the social integration of the Asian community

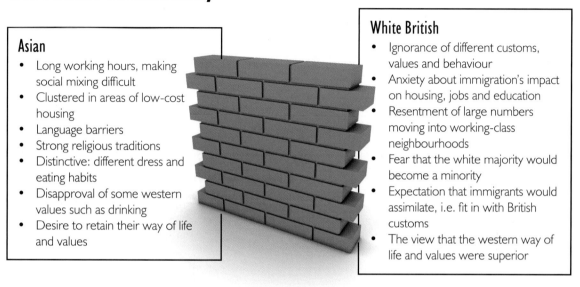

Asian
- Long working hours, making social mixing difficult
- Clustered in areas of low-cost housing
- Language barriers
- Strong religious traditions
- Distinctive: different dress and eating habits
- Disapproval of some western values such as drinking
- Desire to retain their way of life and values

White British
- Ignorance of different customs, values and behaviour
- Anxiety about immigration's impact on housing, jobs and education
- Resentment of large numbers moving into working-class neighbourhoods
- Fear that the white majority would become a minority
- Expectation that immigrants would assimilate, i.e. fit in with British customs
- The view that the western way of life and values were superior

Writing about post-war Muslim immigrants, Humayun Ansari states:

> They had come to Britain to raise their living standards, not to change their way of life.
>
> (H. Ansari, *The Infidel Within: Muslims in Britain since 1800* (2009))

By the 1970s many Asian families, especially the younger generation, had adapted to British life. Ansari comments that as individuals many were 'well integrated' but as communities they remained 'detached'. In terms of working lives, in language and in male dress, the Asian community accepted British norms. Yet they were keen to retain and protect their religion, family values and social habits. With hindsight, this degree of social integration seems a workable compromise for both communities but at the time it caused hostility and accusations of **communalism**.

Just as social integration proved a hard struggle so did political recognition and equal rights under the law. In early April 1968 the Labour Government introduced its **Race Relations Bill** which tackled racial discrimination in housing and jobs. One of Mr Jolly's local MPs, Enoch Powell, had strongly opposed the Sikh campaign and now focused his anger on this new Bill. In April 1968 Powell delivered one of the most famous speeches in political history, which divided both politicians and the public on the issue of race.

communalism
Over-concentration on religious differences and the fostering of hostility between different religious groups. It was often used to describe the religious strife in India between Hindus, Muslims, Sikhs and Christians

The **Race Relations Bill** was about political recognition of the right to social integration, so like the previous example can be noted on your timeline as a development that covers both aspects.

The name of the speech: Powell always referred to it as the 'Birmingham Speech' but it is generally remembered as the 'Rivers of Blood' speech, although the phrase was not actually used in the speech.

Political context: The arrival of 1000 Kenyan Asians early in the year had prompted Parliament to impose tighter immigration controls in February. In early April 1968 the new Race Relations Bill was introduced.

The political impact of the speech: Powell was expelled from the Shadow Cabinet by Conservative leader Edward Heath and never recovered a mainstream voice in British politics.

Enoch Powell and the 'Rivers of Blood' speech, April 1968

△ Enoch Powell.

Public support for the speech: Opinion polls over the following weeks showed that more than two-thirds of those interviewed supported what he had said about immigrants. Powell himself received more than 100,000 letters with only about 800 opposing his speech. Workers expressed their support for Powell; more than 4000 dock workers went on strike to show their support, the Transport and General Workers' Union sent a petition to Heath and in Wolverhampton brewery workers marched on the Town Hall shouting 'Ted out, Enoch in'. Edward ('Ted') Heath was leader of the Conservative Party.

The impact on race relations: In many mixed-race neighbourhoods, tensions rose in the weeks after the speech. Paul Boateng, a schoolboy in London at the time, stated: 'I was shouted at and spat at and abused in the street for the first time ever, the day after that.' 'That' was Powell's speech.

Public opposition to the speech: Broadsheet (serious, mainly middle class) newspapers condemned it, an editorial of *The Times* branding it an 'evil speech'. University students campaigned vociferously against Powell, heckling and interrupting him or preventing him from speaking at all in the years that followed.

Enoch Powell: Powell was the son of two school teachers who grew up in the Midlands and became a talented scholar, specialising in the classics, that is the study of ancient Greece and Rome. After graduating from Cambridge he became a Professor at Sydney University and then served as a brigadier in the Second World War. He lived in India for some time, returning to the UK to become Conservative MP for Wolverhampton South West in 1950. His political career took off and in 1968 he was shadow (i.e. opposition) spokesman on defence.

The content of the speech: Powell reaffirmed the three central points of Conservative Party immigration policy: stricter controls on entry to the UK, encouragement of voluntary repatriation and equal treatment of immigrants who had settled here. He had made similar points in articles and speeches earlier in the year. He opposed the new Race Relations Bill, arguing it would be used as a weapon against the white community and he predicted serious repercussions unless immigration was reduced.

The place and the audience: Powell made his speech at the Midland Hotel, in the heart of Birmingham, only a short distance from where he went to school. The speech was being made to the Annual General Meeting of leading Conservatives of the area. Unusual for this kind of event, there was a strong press presence and television cameras were there to record it. Powell had told a friend that the speech would 'go up like a rocket' and he knew that his words would be reported in the national press.

■ The historical problem: the use of language

Racism and racialism

The word 'racist' was not widely used in Britain until the 1970s. Heath described Powell's speech as 'racialist in tone'. The word 'racialist' is similar to racist in that it means someone who believes that there are differences between races and some are superior to others. 'Racist' is a word that became widely used in the USA in the 1960s with the black civil rights movement.

Was Powell a racist?

From the perspective of the twenty-first century, few people reading Powell's speech would have any hesitation in calling Powell a racist. Yet it is worth remembering that:

• Powell was a great admirer of Indian culture and customs and spoke fluent Urdu. He had witnessed the eruption of violence in India in 1947–48 when half a million people had lost their lives due to racial and religious conflict.

• In 1959 Powell had spoken passionately in the House of Commons in protest at the deaths of African detainees in British-ruled Kenya. He had strongly opposed the suggestion, made by some of his fellow Conservatives, that different standards could be applied to British and African citizens.

• As health minister in the early 1960s, Powell had initiated a recruitment drive in the West Indies to redress employment shortages in the National Health Service.

Powell had a complex range of views on racial matters which arose from his upbringing, education and experience. Lots of people of his generation, including both my grandmothers, shared many of his views.

As citizens of the twenty-first century, we would condemn the attitudes conveyed in Powell's speech as racist. But as historians, we need to use language carefully and think about the purpose of studying history. It is not helpful to use modern-day ideas to judge people of the past, for example, to call Henry VIII 'sexist'. We study the Tudor monarchs to try to understand the values and attitudes of that time and this means we have to think beyond some of the ideas of our own era. This does not mean that we think it was right for Henry to have affairs outside marriage and then to cut off his wife's head when she did the same!

So why did Powell's speech cause such a furore? Looking at the words he spoke makes this clearer.

Extracts from Powell's speech

A A week or two ago I fell into conversation with a constituent, a middle-aged, quite ordinary working man employed in one of our nationalised industries. After a sentence or two about the weather, he suddenly said: 'If I had the money to go, I wouldn't stay in this country.' I made some deprecatory reply to the effect that even this government wouldn't last for ever; but he took no notice, and continued: 'I have three children, all of them been through grammar school and two of them married now, with family. I shan't be satisfied till I have seen them all settled overseas. In this country in 15 or 20 years' time the black man will have the whip hand over the white man.'

I can already hear the chorus of execration. How dare I say such a horrible thing? How dare I stir up trouble and inflame feelings by repeating such a conversation?

The answer is that I do not have the right not to do so. Here is a decent, ordinary fellow Englishman, who in broad daylight in my own town says to me, his Member of Parliament, that his country will not be worth living in for his children.

B It almost passes belief that at this moment 20 or 30 additional immigrant children are arriving from overseas in Wolverhampton alone every week — and that means 15 or 20 additional families a decade or two hence. Those whom the gods wish to destroy, they first make mad. We must be mad, literally mad, as a nation to be permitting the annual inflow of some 50,000 dependants, who are for the most part the material of the future growth of the immigrant-descended population. It is like watching a nation busily engaged in heaping up its own funeral pyre. So insane are we that we actually permit unmarried persons to immigrate for the purpose of founding a family with spouses and fiancés whom they have never seen …

C I am going to allow just one of those hundreds of people to speak for me:
'Eight years ago in a respectable street in Wolverhampton a house was sold to a Negro. Now only one white (a woman old aged pensioner) lives there. This is her story. She lost her husband and both her sons in the war. So she turned her seven-roomed house, her only asset, into a boarding house. She worked hard and did well, paid off her mortgage and began to put something by for her old age.

This phrase is a direct reference to the days of **slavery** with a suggestion of the reversal of the 'natural' state of white supremacy over blacks.

Both these comments are attributed to people from Powell's constituency but he has chosen to repeat their words in his speech.

Powell was a great scholar of **ancient Greece and Rome** and those educated in grammar and public schools at that time would have shared his knowledge. He uses these classical references to give his speech intellectual authority.

It was not what Powell said that caused a problem for politicians or public, it was the way he said it. Defending his sacking of Powell, Edward Heath commented that 'I don't believe that the great majority of British people share Mr Powell's way of putting his views in his speech'.

What does Powell's speech tell us about political recognition and social integration by 1968?

- In 1968 there was considerable agreement about race and immigration between the main political parties: that the level of immigration must be reduced and efforts needed to be made to address the racial tensions. The Commonwealth Immigration Act, passed in February, which insisted on a 'close connection' with the UK gave preferential entry to white immigrants yet was passed by 372 votes with only 62 against.

Then the immigrants moved in. With growing fear, she saw one house after another taken over. The quiet street became a place of noise and confusion. Regretfully, her white tenants moved out.

'The day after the last one left, she was awakened at 7a.m. by two Negroes who wanted to use her 'phone to contact their employer. When she refused, as she would have refused any stranger at such an hour, she was abused and feared she would have been attacked but for the chain on her door. Immigrant families have tried to rent rooms in her house, but she always refused. Her little store of money went, and after paying rates, she has less than £2 per week. She went to apply for a rate reduction and was seen by a young girl, who on hearing she had a seven-roomed house, suggested she should let part of it. When she said the only people she could get were Negroes, the girl said, 'Racial prejudice won't get you anywhere in this country.' So she went home.

'The telephone is her lifeline. Her family pays the bill, and helps her out as best they can. Immigrants have offered to buy her house – at a price which the prospective landlord would be able to recover from his tenants in weeks, or at most a few months. She is becoming afraid to go out. Windows are broken. She finds excreta pushed through her letter box. When she goes to the shops, she is followed by children, charming, wide-grinning piccaninnies. They cannot speak English, but one word they know. 'Racialist', they chant. When the new Race Relations Bill is passed, this woman is convinced she will go to prison. And is she so wrong? I begin to wonder.'

The other dangerous delusion from which those who are wilfully or otherwise blind to realities suffer, is summed up in the word 'integration'. To be integrated into a population means to become, for all practical purposes, indistinguishable from its other members.

D For these dangerous and divisive elements the legislation proposed in the Race Relations Bill is the very **pabulum** they need to flourish. Here is the means of showing that the immigrant communities can organise to consolidate their members, to agitate and campaign against their fellow citizens, and to overawe and dominate the rest with the legal weapons which the ignorant and the ill-informed have provided. As I look ahead, I am filled with foreboding; like the Roman, I seem to see 'the River Tiber foaming with much blood'.

The word **'piccaninny'** is an offensive term for black children that was used in America.

Powell uses **shocking language** to make an impact.

pabulum
Environment in which ideas can flourish

- Most politicians agreed that immigrants who had settled in the UK needed protection from prejudice and ill-treatment although not all agreed that legal changes were the best means to achieve this.

- Working-class families were the most likely to live in mixed-race neighbourhoods and many were worried about the impact of immigration on jobs, education and housing. Some felt threatened by measures to give ethnic minorities equal legal rights.

- The use of inflammatory racial language was unacceptable to most people at this time.

■ Use this summary to make notes on your timeline.

Have Britain's police helped or hindered the path of multi-culturalism from the 1970s onwards?

In the goals of both social integration and political recognition, the police play a crucial role. On the streets they are the symbols of government authority, enforcing and interpreting the law. Their relationship with Britain's ethnic minorities has often been a good barometer of the progress in race relations.

■ Consider what this case tells you about political recognition of the rights of immigrants at this time and make a note on your timeline.

David Oluwale was a victim of institutional racism. His body was found floating in the River Aire, near Leeds, in May 1969. Two police officers had regularly made this homeless Nigerian the focus of their bullying and humiliating attacks, finally beating him to death. But Oluwale's case reveals more than cruel victimisation by two individuals. More than once, station officials filled in his nationality on his paperwork as 'Wog'. When his assailants were tried, much was made of Oluwale's mental illness and criminal record and no positive witnesses were heard. It was no surprise that the judge ordered the charge of manslaughter to be dropped and the offenders got off lightly.

Problems in relations between police and the immigrant community were identified as early as 1971 when a Select Committee was asked to investigate. They discovered several key problems. The police judged that the black population was more likely to commit crime although this was not statistically true. Resentment by young blacks at perceived police harassment and at their own social and economic disadvantage were contributory problems. Very often a cycle of poor communication on the streets led to conflict:

A policeman's mode of address is resented by a black youth sensitive to insult; the youth replies with what the policeman sees as insolence, often accompanied by gesticulation; the policeman counters with what the youth sees as hostile formality. Neither understands the other's point of view; each sees the other as a threat. The youth says he is being picked on because he is black and the policeman is immediately in a dilemma. If he takes firm action he can be accused of racial bias by black people, if he doesn't he is open to the same accusation by white people.

(J. Solomos, *Race and Racism in Britain* (2003))

This cycle of misunderstanding persisted in subsequent years as shown by two landmark reports, the Scarman Report and the Macpherson Report.

A shift can be seen from Scarman, who blamed the conflict on a mix of social problems and insensitive policing, to Macpherson who concentrated on the police service itself. Scarman's recommendations were only partially accepted by Prime Minister Thatcher, who criticised Brixton families for their lack of discipline. But general attitudes were, indeed, slowly shifting. In contrast the Labour government endorsed most of Macpherson's recommendations, passing a new Race Relations Act in 2000 which made all public agencies tackle discrimination in their work.

The Scarman Report 1981

Context

A tense relationship between police and the black community in Brixton escalated into a full-scale riot leading to the destruction of 145 premises and more than 250 injuries.

Main findings

- The riots were a spontaneous outbreak of resentment against the police led mainly by black youths.
- Black families living in Brixton suffered numerous social, economic and educational disadvantages, especially high unemployment.
- The relationship between police and community was poor, especially due to the use of 'hard' policing methods such as stop and search powers.
- Some aspects of West Indian family life such as working mothers and absent fathers increased social disadvantage.
- Some junior policemen were prejudiced and could infect others with their views, but on the whole the force was not racist.

The Macpherson Report 1999

Context

Stephen Lawrence, a black A Level student, was stabbed to death by white youths as he waited at a bus stop in South London in 1993. The police failed to bring the suspects to justice.

Main findings

- Stephen's friend (with him at the time of the murder) and family had not been treated with respect because of their racial background.
- The initial police response to the murder had been incompetent and led to the failure to bring a prosecution.
- The police were 'institutionally racist', defined by Macpherson as '… the collective failure of an organisation to provide an appropriate and professional service to people because of their colour, culture or ethnic origin'.

This was clear political recognition that all British institutions needed to publicly endorse equal treatment for all citizens regardless of race or background.

Since Macpherson there was increased recruitment of ethnic minority officers and determined efforts by the police to build better community relations. A public survey of 2001 stated that only 5 per cent regarded the police as racist. Fifteen police forces, however, still had no black or Asian officers and black people were five times more likely to be stopped in London than whites. Some argued that Macpherson had gone too far, and William Hague, a leading Conservative politician, linked a rise in street crime to a reluctance to stop potential criminals because of police fear of being accused of racism.

Serious disturbances took place in Bradford, Burnley and Oldham between the Pakistani community and the police in the summer of 2001. In Bradford alone damage was estimated at £27 million and 300 police officers were injured. While the Labour politician David Blunkett praised the tough sentences meted out to the mainly Asian Muslim offenders, Fair Justice for All campaigners focused on the provocation by right-wing groups and heavy-handed policing lying behind the riots. For them it was just another instance of institutional racism aimed at a community still suffering social and economic disadvantage. These clashes suggest that progress towards social integration was still slow.

The police and the travelling community

Relations between the travelling community, resident population and police have also been troubled over the last 50 years.

PC Steve Dean, of Gypsy background and with a long police career of 30 years, suffered abuse from police when growing up but went on to become a leading advisor on relations between police and the travelling community. In 2005 he said in an interview:

'Not only could we offer support to each other, but also break down some of the misunderstandings surrounding the Gypsy and Traveller community. One side of my family is Gypsy and I am very proud of my heritage. My grandparents were lovely people. But it is important to stress that this is about equality and equal treatment. Some minority groups want better treatment than others. It is very important that that doesn't happen as it just results in conflict. Equality has to mean just that.'

Did Britain become a multi-cultural society in the years 1970–2005?

His children were 'more British than the British themselves' asserted Jaffer Kapasi in an interview in 2002. Kapasi, now a prominent Leicestershire businessman, arrived with his family from Uganda in 1972 with just a suitcase of belongings, having been expelled at short notice by the dictator Idi Amin. Not sharing his own African memories, his children felt that Britain was their home.

Shafiq Uddin's six children would probably share these feelings. Their father arrived in London from Bangladesh in the late 1950s, had a long, successful career as a Wimpy bar manager and married a white East End girl. Uddin said proudly of his children: 'They all own their own houses, except my young one. None of them is unemployed. All have been working since leaving school.' His wife converted to Islam and his children have been brought up as Muslims. But four out of five of his children have married outside his own Bangladeshi community.

Second-generation migrants tended to be better educated, more integrated and better off than their parents. But this did not necessarily mean greater social harmony. They are also often more confident and assertive. Sikh and Muslim girls have challenged the law on their right to wear religious dress or emblems at school. David Lammy who grew up in Tottenham, North London, wrote:

> My parents' contemporaries had been respectful of authority, even when it was less respectful of them. The generation born in Britain but still not accepted by it was starkly different.

The 2001 census showed that 35 per cent of ethnic minorities of working age in the UK were born here. How far has this growing proportion of second- and third-generation immigrants achieved social integration and political recognition? The following two regional studies reveal contrasting experiences of how mixed racial communities have developed.

The city of Leicester: the success of social integration?

'In your own interests and those of your family you should … not come to Leicester.' These were the words in Leicester City Council's advertisement placed in a leading Ugandan newspaper in 1972. City councillors and even local Asian leaders were agreed: services would be overstretched and the already active National Front would greet them with hostility.

But the expelled Ugandan Asians did settle in Leicester and joined a pre-existing Asian community of 10,000. By 1981 more than a fifth of Leicester's population were of Indian descent, mostly Hindus and Sikhs, including Ugandan and Kenyan Asians. It is predicted that Leicester will be the first British city to have a non-white majority, probably by 2015 (it was 50.6% white in the 2011 census).

Leicester has become a genuinely diverse and culturally rich place to live. The coffee kiosk at its main station welcomes customers in four Asian languages. It has numerous Hindu temples, Sikh gurdwaras and Muslim mosques and various different religious festivals are colourfully celebrated in the streets. There are two local Asian radio stations and three cinemas that specialise in Bollywood films. Leicester elected Britain's first Asian MP and by 2006 a third of the city's councillors came from ethnic minority backgrounds. There have been racist incidents, divisions between communities and some resentment in poorer white working-class neighbourhoods but these have never escalated into violence or abuse as in other cities. The former Ugandan Asians are among Leicester's most prosperous citizens and in 2002 the city council made a formal apology for the newspaper advert of 1972.

The reasons for Leicester's successful multi-culturalism are debatable. A former Lord Mayor, Councillor Bhatti, attributes it to a policy of 'civic engagement' – race relations committees, business organisations, sponsorship of festivals and active participation in local politics. The city council has a long record of supporting the construction of places of worship and community centres. The nature of Leicester's immigrants may also be significant with a high proportion of **twice migrants** who spoke several languages, had already adjusted to foreign ways of life and had a mixed heritage themselves. Furthermore, they were generally better educated and more financially independent than other migrants, many of them having had properties and businesses before their arrival. The upward mobility of the immigrant population has led to greater dispersal: Le Goff's research has shown that Leicester's ethnic minorities live 'in a mixed multi-cultural suburban landscape' rather than in separate neighbourhoods. Many of the city's population share a military heritage; a museum wing devoted to the Royal Leicestershire Regiment opened in 2007 with innumerable contributions from local veteran Gurkhas, Sikhs and Punjabis. All these factors may have helped to build a generally harmonious mixed society.

twice migrants
People who have emigrated from their own country, settled in another and then moved on again. Ugandan Asians are examples of 'twice migrants'

Huguenot
French Protestants who fled persecution in the seventeenth century

Sylhet
An area of Bangladesh (formerly East Pakistan)

△ Brick Lane mosque.

London's East End: the problems of social integration?

The Jamme Masjid mosque at 59 Brick Lane is a useful symbol of the East End's constantly changing religious mix. It started as a **Huguenot** church, served as a Methodist chapel and then a Jewish synagogue before its final transformation. From 1976 it has been serving a large Bangladeshi Muslim community.

The outbreak of war in 1971 led many men to flee East Pakistan and join the existing Bangladeshi community in London's East End, with their families coming over later. Often with limited education or English, they worked in low-paid jobs in textiles and workshops and lived in overcrowded basements and attics. The strong **Sylhet** tradition of cooking led many to start setting up their own cafes or work as cooks and waiters in restaurants. Now the Brick Lane area is famous for its rich mix of Bangladeshi cafes, shops and restaurants and is sometimes called 'Bangla town'.

Like the Jewish population before them, the Bangladeshi community have suffered harassment and violence from right-wing groups. In the 1970s they were the victims of white skinhead gangs and National Front activists. Bengali children had to have police protection on their way to and from school and special fire-proof letter boxes were fitted to houses and flats. The violence culminated in the murder of 25-year-old Altab Ali on his way home from work in 1978 by three teenagers. They left a message on the wall next to the victim saying 'We're back'.

The East End community did not simply accept this treatment. The Bangladesh Youth Movement was founded in 1976 as a self-help group for young Bengalis in the Tower Hamlets area. National Front marches were met with strong resistance. There were weekend sit-downs in Brick Lane. After the murder of Altab Ali, 7000 Bengali protesters marched on Downing Street and political organisations campaigned for fairer policing and better rights. In 1978, 100,000 people marched from Trafalgar Square to take part in a vast Rock Against Racism concert in Hackney's Victoria Park.

The Bangladeshi population in London's East End remained one of the most segregated and disadvantaged immigrant groups. They were lower paid and more likely to suffer unemployment, ill health and discrimination than other communities. Furthermore, racist groups continued to be active both politically and on the streets. From 1993 the anti-immigration British National Party has won seats in local council elections in various East End boroughs and in the 1990s racist incidents actually increased.

In the twenty-first century the East End has continued to be a diverse and cosmopolitan community, now including new arrivals from Somalia and Eastern Europe. The mix of vibrant curry restaurants and lively street markets, poverty and racial divisions partly reflects its history in one of the more deprived regions of London. The decline in the docks, the textile and garment trades and the pressure on housing stock may explain why better off Jewish families moved out and Bangladeshis moved in. Right-wing and even racist politics have had a voice in the East End since the 1930s so the activities of the National Front and the BNP may be unsurprising. Although there are growing signs of improvement, lower levels of education and employment for all East Enders have also played a part in continuing resentments and tensions.

Review: How far has Britain achieved multi-culturalism?

'There must be increased pessimism about how far different communities in our nation can ever be integrated or want to be' stated an editorial in the *Daily Telegraph* in May 1989. This judgement was triggered by the publication of *The Satanic Verses*, a novel by the Indian-born writer, Salman Rushdie. Although it received favourable literary reviews, the book caused an outcry in the Muslim community for its depiction of the life of Muhammed. In Iran, a **fatwa** was issued directing Muslims to kill the author and he was given police protection. An apology from Rushdie for the offence he had caused did not lead to the fatwa's withdrawal. Many Muslim organisations rallied against Rushdie's work, arguing that the **blasphemy laws** should be extended to cover other faiths. The book was symbolically burnt in Bradford and demonstrations took place in cities such as Leicester and Birmingham. For many Muslims this episode was a turning point, Inayat Bunglawala stating:

> It brought Muslims together. Before that they had been identified as ethnic communities but *The Satanic Verses* brought them together and helped develop a British Muslim identity …

Since the Rushdie affair, the division between Muslim and non-Muslim Britain seems only to have widened. There have been clashes over the wearing of the veil, forced marriages and the preaching of radical fundamentalism in some mosques. Most shocking of all, in 2005 suicide bombers attacked Londoners on their way to work, killing 52 people. Their leader, Mohammad Sidique Khan, was a classroom assistant from Leeds with a baby daughter. He was born in the UK and a product of a multi-cultural education system.

Muslims who advocated or used violence were always a small minority of the British Islamic community. But the Rushdie affair, and the events following it, revealed a conflict at the heart of multi-culturalism. The desire to respect minority faiths, traditions and cultures could, and often did, clash with the desire to protect traditional liberal values such as equality for women and freedom of the press. In the twenty-first century, it seemed, the limits of both social integration and political recognition had been reached.

fatwa
A legal pronouncement made by an Islamic scholar. In some cases this can instruct Muslims to use violence against an enemy of Islam. The fatwa against Rushdie was issued by the Ayatollah Khomeini of Iran. Three of Rushdie's publishers and translators were attacked in 1991

blasphemy laws
Attacks on the Christian faith but not other faiths were illegal until these laws were repealed in 2008

> What does the Rushdie case suggest about political recognition? Consider the traditional political rights to free speech and the rights of the Muslim community to equal treatment under the law.

When, if ever, did Britain become a multi-cultural society?

How serious this conflict was depends largely on the definition of multi-culturalism adopted.

Lord Parekh, Professor of Political Philosophy, and a supporter of multi-culturalism:

'Multiculturalism basically means that no culture is perfect or represents the best life and that it can therefore benefit from a critical dialogue with other cultures. In this sense multiculturalism requires that all cultures should be open, self-critical, and interactive in their relations with each other.'

Kenneth Minogue, Professor of Political Science, and a critic of multi-culturalism:

'The doctrine is that we must, on pain of committing discriminatory racism, regard every individual, and every culture in which individuals participate, as being equally valuable. Indeed, as the doctrine develops, we must not only share this opinion. We must regard people of all cultures with equal affection, employ them, make friends with them, promote them and include them in everything we do, in proportion to their numbers in the population.'

These two quotations illustrate how different interpretations of multi-culturalism can be. For the purposes of this enquiry, multi-culturalism has been defined as a positive acceptance of ethnic and cultural diversity, respect for differing faiths, and equal legal and political rights for all British citizens.

Immigrant names on the New Year's Honours list, curry cookbooks in the bookshops and white participants in the Notting Hill Carnival only provide evidence of what has been called 'celebratory' or 'consumer' multi-culturalism, not proof of an integrated and mutually respectful society. In other words, Britons publicly enjoy aspects of our multi-ethnic society, making the nation look tolerant and mixed, while behind the scenes, in ordinary neighbourhoods, racism persists. In 2004 a survey showed that 94 per cent of white people in Britain had 'few or no ethnic minority friends'. A year later, Trevor Phillips, the head of the Commission for Racial Equality, warned that Britain was 'sleepwalking' into racial and religious segregation as impoverished minorities congregated in Britain's poorest neighbourhoods. In Barking, East London, the anti-immigrant British National Party won nearly 17 per cent of the vote and increased its following nationally in the 2005 elections.

Yet it would be wrong to ignore substantial changes in public attitudes and national culture. Modern British sport, music and media are all the product of years of ethnic and cultural mixing. In twenty-first century Britain racist language is not tolerated on our television screens or in football stands. If Learie Constantine wanted to book into a London hotel in 2005, he would have been told he could stay as long as he wanted.

Now look back on the four measures of multi-culturalism set out at the start of the chapter and your completed timeline. Use these as a way of reaching your own developed conclusions about when, if ever, Britain became truly multi-cultural.

Multi-culturalism and Britishness: the British Airways' tailfin design

Advocates of multi-culturalism do not regard the growing diversity of faiths, languages and cultures in Britain as a threat to the national identity of the country. They argue that Britain has a long history of immigration, that diversity enriches British culture and that British institutions are robust enough to cope with new arrivals. Celebration of Hindu or Muslim festivals does not mean that Christmas is underplayed.

Opponents feel that multi-culturalism has undermined national pride and unity so that citizens no longer have a strong sense of what it means to be British. They call for a stronger emphasis on British history, language, religion and culture and unabashed celebration of British traditions such as Guy Fawkes Day.

The case of British Airways' tailfins reveals different views in the late 1990s

In 1997 British Airways' boss, Bob Ayling, decided to 'lose some of our old-fashioned Britishness and take on board some of the new British traits'. The traditional Union flag on his aeroplanes' tailfins was replaced with new designs from a range of ethnic arts and images. The change was a flop. The new designs were deeply unpopular with the public, and former Prime Minister Thatcher hated them. Within two years they were being replaced by the familiar Union flag and by 2001 they had disappeared. The company's experiment with multi-culturalism was short lived.

△ Some of the new design BA tailfins.

△ The Union flag tailfin.

A closer look at political speeches

The immigration debate in the spring of 1968

Broadly speaking the purpose of a political speech is to win support. Speeches are usually constructed much like essays, with clear opening points, a logical argument and a strong summing up. Unlike essays, though, they are addressed to a live audience. They need to hold attention and appeal to their listeners. The nature of a speech will also be greatly affected by the intended audience and the context of the times. Lots of politicians made speeches about the controversial issue of immigration in 1968, but Powell's is the only one that is remembered now. Using this speech as an example, we can consider the nature of speeches as evidence and the problems they pose.

Below are two extracts from political speeches about immigration made in 1968:

A It is not about keeping Britain white. It is about keeping Britain honest. That is the whole burden of my case. We are not divided in wanting to keep the essential characteristics of the British nation, fair play, fair mindedness and good neighbourliness. We all appreciate that these will go unless we check unbridled immigration.

B I would add only one very personal experience. When I represented another constituency before going to Torquay, where I make no pretence that a great racial problem exists, I helped to guarantee the mortgage of a young couple who came to me for help in buying a house over twenty years ago for about £1700. Because of conditions for which they are not responsible, the area in which they live has had a massive immigrant element injected. The last time I heard from them I learned that when the husband, nearing the end of his working life, wanted to sell his house, the highest offer he could get was £450 from one immigrant, despite rising property values over the past fifteen years.

These are facts which no amount of talking about one's conscience will alter. It is unreal to deny that this sort of thing exists. We all know many more such examples, which are the real causes of the tension which many of us know.

These two extracts are from Conservative MPs talking in the House of Commons debate on immigration in February 1968. It is noticeable how similar their comments are to Powell's 'Rivers of Blood' oration yet they did not cause a stir. Powell's strong language partly explains this, but not completely. It is also explained by the context of these speeches.

At that time there was no radio or television recording allowed in Parliament although newspaper journalists could make notes and all speeches were eventually published in the parliamentary journal *Hansard*. Strict rules applied about the behaviour and language that MPs could use and the atmosphere at this time was often like a gentlemen's debating club. The speaker of the House of Commons would select those allowed to speak; usually those with responsibilities or expertise in that area. The Immigration Bill in February 1968 attracted majority support, including all the leading Conservatives. Powell did not contribute to this debate.

Instead, Powell expressed his views on immigration in the public arena, alerting journalists in advance so that they could make a live recording and reach a much wider audience than regional Conservative activists. Speaking on home turf, he knew he had the support of the local party and press. Some commentators, such as Paul Foot, believe the main purpose behind the speech was to advance his political career by showing he was more in touch with public opinion than the Conservative leader, Ted Heath.

So when considering political speeches as evidence, it is important to think carefully about the:

- intended audience
- purpose of the speech
- venue
- timing.

All of these might affect the way you interpret the words spoken and the weight you place upon them as evidence.

◁ A black man walks past graffiti supporting Enoch Powell, London, 1968.

3 Ain't misbehaving? Why did teenagers' lives seem to be changing?

What was influencing the young?

Mark Feld becomes Marc Bolan

Early 1960s	Marc Bolan as a **mod** in 1962 (photo top left): Wearing an impeccable mod outfit, Marc aged only fourteen was featured in a magazine article. He was obsessed with clothes. As a working-class lad in a council house, he afforded his fashion tastes by stealing and selling-on motor bikes and jeans. At this stage he was playing guitar with a **skiffle band** and was an admirer of the British pop idol Cliff Richard and the American star Chuck Berry.
1967	Having left school at fifteen, Marc worked as a model before joining the pop band, John's Children. His song 'Desdemona' was banned by the BBC due to the chorus line 'Lift up your skirt and fly'. While with the band, Bolan gained a reputation for wild behaviour on stage and for excessive drinking.
1969–70	Marc Bolan as a psychedelic hippie (photo below left). As part of the band Tyrannosaurus Rex, Bolan's musical career took off. His own distinctive style of music, using a vintage acoustic guitar, was widely admired, leading to concerts, airtime on Radio 1 and several hit singles. A leader of the hippie movement, Bolan wrote mystical poetry, grew his hair long and experimented with drugs.
1971–72	Renaming his band T Rex, Bolan was a prominent figure of the 'Glam Rock' movement, wearing feather boas and glitter on his face. His reputation for challenging lyrics continued with his 1972 song 'Children of the Revolution'. It is estimated that he earned around £2 million from his music in 1972, a fortune in those days. From 1973 his career began to fade, possibly due to an increasing cocaine habit. He died in a car crash in 1977.

pop music Short for popular music, this is music that is often simple and repetitive often with romantic lyrics and easy to dance to

rock music Music with vocals but also a strong back beat with use of guitar, drums and bass

subculture A group within a national culture whose members share distinctive behaviour, dress and styles

counter culture A cultural movement or group that rejects the values and tastes of mainstream society

Bolan's life was full of contradictions. He was a pop star, a millionaire, a rebel and a trendsetter. He was happy to make money from big commercial contracts and to have his music played by the BBC. Yet his attraction to young people was partly his rebellious image and lyrics. His sense of style and his musical output changed with the years; a blend of contemporary culture and creative individualism. His story showed how talent and ambition could win fame for a working-class boy. Yet his drugs and drinking made him a poor role model.

Was Bolan's life moulded by commercial and cultural pressures or did he make his own choices? How far did he influence his fans? These are impossible questions to answer. The interplay of culture, commerce, the media and Bolan himself are hard to disentangle. His music and image drew on previous traditions and his own creations were copied and developed by others.

This is also true of the younger generation in general. They were certainly affected by TV programmes, teen magazines and American pop and film idols. Yet some youth movements, like the hippies and punks, rejected commercialism. Music and image went hand in hand for mods, rockers and punks and ready cash helped young people to indulge their tastes and create their own styles. In your study of influences on modern youth, you need to be aware of this complex inter-relationship.

mod
A teenage subculture of the 1960s (see p.46)

skiffle band
A band, usually of amateur musicians, sometimes playing homemade instruments

---

■ Enquiry Focus: Why did teenagers' lives seem to be changing?

In the 1950s and 1960s many people talked about youth rebellion or the 'teen revolution'. Certainly the older generation thought that young people had changed and many articles were written about the problems they presented. Looking back, many historians wonder if the changes were as radical as they seemed at the time. Yet they still acknowledge that the post-war generation was different from their parents in several fundamental ways. Some of the more obvious changes are summarised on page 42 but there were more subtle changes too. Teenagers developed a stronger sense of their own culture and identity, they deliberately adopted music and dress styles that their parents disliked and their challenges to authority were more overtly political and organised. None of these developments was completely new but they were more apparent in this generation.

What makes a teenager tick? Certainly, their families influence them. As they mature their friends become increasingly important. Teachers and schools may affect what they know and how they behave. They will adopt styles and tastes they hear on the radio and see in the media. Their own environments will partly mould them as will their spending power. It's not going to be possible in this chapter to consider all these influences but that does not mean the omissions don't matter. But as this chapter concentrates on what made the young in these decades *seem* so different, the main focus will be five growing influences in the post-war decades that people at the time considered important:

1 Gangs and violence – the emergence of teen youth groups such as mods and rockers and their influence on the behaviour of young people.

2 Americanisation – the growing impact of American culture and language in Britain.

3 Teenage spending power – the growth in young people's incomes and their increased freedom to spend it as they wished.

4 Rock and pop music – the explosion in popular music and its impact on young people's behaviour and ideas.

5 Left-wing politics – the growth of protest movements such as the Campaign for Nuclear Disarmament and university demonstrations.

When finishing your study of each of these topics, complete the following tasks:

a Make notes to identify the impact of each influence.

b Explain why some people saw this impact as i) positive ii) negative.

c Consider how far teenagers' lives were really affected by each influence.

Key changes in the lives of young people

Changes in music

These decades saw an explosion in new forms of popular music. It was the rock and roll era and the years of The Beatles.

Some highlights:

- Development of rock and pop in the USA: Elvis released 'Heartbreak Hotel' in 1956 and Buddy Holly completed a hugely popular UK tour in 1958.
- The Beatles had their first number 1 in 1963 with 'Please Please Me' and continued to dominate the charts until 1970.
- The BBC's Radio 1 was launched in 1967 to cater for the thirst for rock and pop music that had previously only been provided by pirate radio stations.

Changes in education

Young people stayed in education much longer than their parents had.

- Compulsory secondary education: The Butler Education Act of 1944 set the school leaving age at fifteen and this was extended to sixteen in 1973.
- Expansion of universities: There was a massive increase in the number of students attending university between 1961 and 1969, rising from 200,000 to 390,000.

Changes in the law

Young people were recognised earlier as independent citizens but their behaviour also presented new challenges.

- National Service: After the war young men had to serve for a period of up to two years in the armed services. This ended in 1960.
- In 1969 the voting age was lowered from 21 to 18.
- As drugs emerged as a serious issue, the Misuse of Drugs Act was passed in 1971 to impose heavier penalties on their use.

Changes in employment

For most of the period from 1945 to 1973, Britain enjoyed full employment meaning that unemployment was consistently below 3 per cent. In the mid-1950s the unemployment rate fell as low as 1 per cent. This meant that school leavers could easily find jobs and switch employment to get the best wages and conditions. There was a full range of opportunities in skilled and semi-skilled positions around the country from old industries such as in textile mills and shipyards to the booming car industry or consumer goods. Although in the 1940s there was a government-imposed pay freeze, from 1950 onwards wages began to rise and young people living at home had money to spend.

Did gangs and groups make young people violent? (1)

◁ A typical sunny day on Margate Beach in the 1960s.

There was Dad asleep in a deckchair and Mum making sandcastles with the children, when the 1964 boys took over the beaches at Margate and Brighton yesterday and smeared the traditional postcard scene with blood and violence.

(*Daily Express*, 19 May 1964)

What happened in Margate on the Whitsun bank holiday weekend in 1964? The newspapers reported that this quiet seaside resort was overrun with wild teenagers; gangs of mods and rockers, who were set on violence and destruction. Innocent old ladies were terrorised and deckchairs were hurled across the sands as hundreds of armed youths turned the beach into a battleground. When sentencing the offenders, local magistrate Dr George Simpson condemned the 'long-haired, mentally unstable, petty little hoodlums, these **sawdust Caesars**, who can only find courage like rats, in hunting in packs, who came to Margate with the avowed intent of interfering with the life and property of its inhabitants'.

sawdust Caesars
People who think they are powerful and important but in reality are insignificant

◁ Margate Beach in 1964.

43

But a closer study of the facts make this version of events look less convincing:

- An estimated 400 youths were present at Margate, of whom 65 were arrested and 47 convicted in court (around 10 per cent).

- There were only three convictions for violence: two stabbings and one man being dropped onto a flower bed.

- Fifty deckchairs were damaged – not an unusual number for a busy bank holiday weekend.

- The most common offence was using threatening behaviour and obstructing the police.

- Almost all the victims were police or youths, not members of the general public.

- The estimated damage caused was £250 (approximately £3,800 today).

- A survey of 34 youths who appeared in court revealed that 12 regarded themselves as neither mods nor rockers.

- Nearly all the more serious incidents happened in the evening when the families had gone home.

- There is evidence that the press paid teenagers to pose for photos of them misbehaving.

- Few teenagers at Margate had long hair. Mods were well known for the neatness of their appearance and their short hair styles.

Stanley Cohen has explained, in his book *Folk Devils and Moral Panics*, how the press often sensationalise news stories, playing upon public anxieties to create interest, increase sales and whip up a bigger story. The Margate magistrate told news reporters that the event was evidence of a problem with British youth of 'colossal national proportions', escalating fear of an epidemic of violence and lawlessness around the country. In reality the seaside disturbances of 1964 did not develop into any significant increases in youth delinquency or misbehaviour.

In the 1960s, teenagers were the particular focus of attention. Dominic Sandbrook explains why:

> Teenagers in the 1960s were iconic figures, not only because of what they did, but because they personified so many of the issues of the day, from the rise of mass entertainment to the new working-class prosperity. As a representative of modernity, energy, sexuality and ambition, the teenager may have captured the hopes of British society, but he also compounded its fears.
>
> (D. Sandbrook, *White Heat: A History of Britain in the Swinging Sixties* (2006))

The historical perspective

The idea that the teenager was 'invented' in the 1950s and 1960s has now been largely discredited and researchers no longer talk of a post-war 'youthquake' or teen revolution. Young people had been in gangs, set their own styles, defied their parents and rioted at football matches long before 1945. The concern about youth at this time fits into a longer term pattern of anxiety about young people.

> I think morals are getting much worse. There were no such girls in my time as there are now. When I was four or five and twenty [24 or 25 years old] my mother would have knocked me down if I had spoken improperly to her.
>
> (Charlotte Kirkman giving evidence to an enquiry into children's employment in the 1840s)

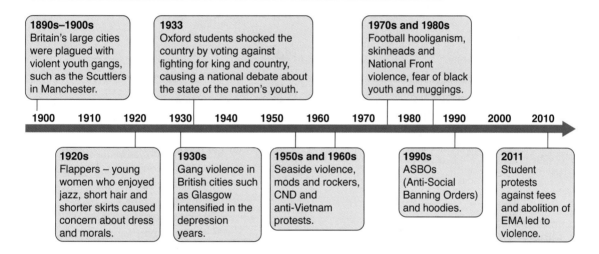

1890s–1900s
Britain's large cities were plagued with violent youth gangs, such as the Scuttlers in Manchester.

1933
Oxford students shocked the country by voting against fighting for king and country, causing a national debate about the state of the nation's youth.

1970s and 1980s
Football hooliganism, skinheads and National Front violence, fear of black youth and muggings.

1920s
Flappers – young women who enjoyed jazz, short hair and shorter skirts caused concern about dress and morals.

1930s
Gang violence in British cities such as Glasgow intensified in the depression years.

1950s and 1960s
Seaside violence, mods and rockers, CND and anti-Vietnam protests.

1990s
ASBOs (Anti-Social Banning Orders) and hoodies.

2011
Student protests against fees and abolition of EMA led to violence.

1956

Is it fair to regard every lad who wears a velvet collar as an anti-social no-good with a bicycle chain up his sleeve?

(Teddy boy, interviewed in the *Daily Mirror*)

2005

I think that banning caps and hoodies is a bad idea because it is saying that whoever wears them, like me, is a bad person.

(Comment on BBC *Newsround* website on the debate on banning the wearing of hoodies in a shopping centre)

Recommended reads

To understand the long history of fear of the younger generation, Geoffrey Pearson's classic *Hooligan: A History of Respectable Fears* (1983) is well worth reading. It shows how many 'modern' youth problems of vandalism, gangs and violence have a long history.

Did gangs and groups make young people violent? (2)

Seventeen-year-old John Beckley was stabbed to death with a flick knife on Clapham Common in 1953. He was killed by a Teddy boy gang calling themselves 'The Plough Boys'. Beckley's crime, it seems, was to insult their clothes. The incident caused an outcry in the press, with the *Daily Mirror* taking the lead in calling for a campaign against juvenile delinquency. The growth of violence was largely attributed to the Teddy boy subculture. A Home Office report on juvenile delinquency in 1960 confirmed that the crime wave was 'associated with certain forms of dress and other social phenomena'.

One distinctive feature of post-war British youth was the emergence of subcultures; teenage groups sharing the same tastes and styles. We have already seen how mods and rockers caused an outcry at the seaside resorts in the 1960s. How far was their misbehaviour a result of the 'gang mentality'? This survey of leading subcultures invites you to consider how far they were a negative influence on the young.

Teddy boys
When? 1950s

Who? White working-class teenagers

What did they get up to? In London area associated with frequent racial attacks and the Notting Hill riots of 1958. Sometimes involved in gang violence and petty theft.

Mods
When? 1960s

Who? Better off working-class teenagers, in skilled or semi-skilled jobs, primarily from London, the suburbs and home counties.

What did they get up to? Hung around suburban dance halls, spending money on drink and clothes. Occasional skirmishes with rocker rivals but, apart from the seaside disturbances of the mid 1960s, rarely violent. Some mods took 'purple hearts' (amphetamines and barbiturate pills). In Glasgow mods were part of the violent gang scene of the 1960s.

Hippies
When? Late 1960s –1970s

Who? Middle-class young people, students

What did they get up to? Often 'dropped out' of society, refusing to conform to the traditions of a nine to five job, marriage and consumer society. Sometimes lived in squats. Often used recreational drugs especially cannabis and LSD and supported the peace movement and **CND**.

Rockers
When? 1960s

Who were they? Working class, usually in more manual and lower paid occupations than their rivals, the mods.

What did they get up to? Raced each other on noisy motorbikes, often gaining speeding tickets. Had occasional fights with mods and, when gathering at petrol stations and transport cafes, intimidated the public.

CND
The Campaign for Nuclear Disarmament, a strong protest movement from the 1950s onwards

Skinheads

When? 1970s

Who? Unskilled white working-class young people

What did they get up to? Tended to hang out in the street and in pubs, intimidating passers-by. Skinheads were directly involved in football violence and right-wing political groups like the National Front. They were responsible for many racial attacks, especially in East London.

Punks

When? 1970s

Who? Disaffected teenagers, saw themselves as outsiders. Punks included working-class youths but also middle-class art college students.

What did they get up to? Punks liked to shock with outrageous hairstyles, unconventional clothes and challenging behaviour. The punk band the Sex Pistols outraged the public by swearing on an ITV programme and by releasing the satirical song 'God Save the Queen' in her silver jubilee year.

Youth deviancy was a powerful feature of post-war society, but these subcultures involved only a minority of young people. Most teenagers were conservative in their outlook and values: a poll of 1978 found that 89 per cent of 15–21-year-olds thought that vandals and hooligans should be dealt with more severely. Even within the subcultural groups, only a tiny fraction were ever convicted of violent crimes. There was a peak in youth crime in the 1950s but this rise was not sustained. The most common offences were theft, vandalism, disorderliness and, later, football hooliganism. Moreover, youth subcultures and misbehaviour were not a new phenomenon. Street violence, gang culture and deviance were features of young people's lives before the Second World War. Links between crime and youth subcultures have proved hard to establish.

While subcultures appeared threatening in their initial stages, they were often moderated when adopted by commerce and the media. Once they became more popular and mainstream, they lost their hard-hitting and more radical edge. Punk, for instance, started as an unruly and defiant working-class attack on the establishment. When punk music was taken up by all the leading record companies, it developed into just another youthful trend in style and music.

The relationship between subcultures and youthful misbehaviour is therefore very hard to prove. Most commentators agree that the danger posed by subcultures was greatly amplified by the media. Yet it is certainly also true that groups of young people, whether football supporters or a skinhead gang, behaved much worse together than they ever did as individuals.

Youth crime statistics need to be treated with great caution as changes in ways of defining and recording crime have a big impact. For instance, the figures suggest that in 1977–78 cases of vandalism *more than doubled*. In fact this was due to a decision to record *all* cases of property damage while previously low-value crimes were omitted.

■ To complete your study of gangs and violence, remember to make notes as suggested on page 41 in order to sum up how far this aspect changed young people's lives.

Were young people spoilt by Uncle Sam? How far was America to blame?

A juke box was a coin-operated music player, designed for public use in bars and cafes. It played a key cultural role in post-war Britain. Teenagers all round the country crowded round them to hear the latest American sounds. Radio broadcasting was controlled by a stuffy BBC and the British Musicians' Union, anxious to limit competition, restricted broadcasting of American rock and roll. Yet they failed to curtail its influence: 'Heartbreak Hotel' by Elvis reached the British Top 20 in 1956 despite rarely being played on the radio.

Yet the juke boxes themselves tell us the limitations of American influence. Adrian Horn's book *Juke Box Britain* (2010) shows how the American model of the juke box was adapted to the British cultural context. Restrictions on imports meant that it was not until 1959 that American machines could be brought in so before this British manufacturers made their own. Economic austerity and a sense of British style led them to reject the brash and colourful US designs and instead create a simpler, modernist style. Yet they still took on board many aspects of the popular American machines. This blend of American and British ideas is a model, in many ways, of the more general influence of the USA on British culture.

In his book, *The Uses of Literacy*, published in 1957, Richard Hoggart described the impact of American-style milk bars on working-class youngsters. Hoggart was an academic who had grown up in a working-class family in Northern England.

▽ A group of Teddy boys congregate around a juke box, 1955.

Girls go to some, but most of the customers are boys aged between fifteen and twenty, with drape suits, picture ties, and an American slouch. Most of them cannot afford a succession of milk shakes, and make cups of tea serve for an hour or two whilst – and this is the main reason for coming – they put copper after copper into the mechanical record-player.

These customers, according to Hoggart, were living in a 'myth world' based on what they took to be the elements of 'American life'. For Hoggart the milk bar and the juke box represented the erosion of traditional British working-class life. British traditions – the pub, playing on the street, gossip on the doorstep – were being replaced by a commercialised American lifestyle. He certainly had a point. Cult Hollywood movies like *Rebel Without a Cause* glamorised American youth and set a trend for denim jeans which has never really died. British teenagers embraced Coca-Cola, Wimpy bars and American slang, and particularly rock and roll, with enthusiasm. American musicians such as Chuck Berry, Buddy Holly, Bob Dylan and, most of all, Elvis, had an enormous following in the UK.

By the mid 1960s, however, Americans were complaining that their own culture was being taken over by 'a British invasion', particularly in fashion and music. It would be hard to argue that American culture was harming British youth, by this stage. The hit British band, The Kinks, were banned from the US due to their violence and bad behaviour and Lennon's comment that 'The Beatles were more popular than Jesus' caused far more offence there than it did in the UK.

Furthermore, other foreign influences were affecting British youth culture. Caribbean immigrants introduced new sounds such as Jamaican Ska. Ska itself was a fusion of Jamaican and American R&B (rhythm and blues), an example of the mixing of musical cultures. This Caribbean musical style was to have a great impact on British culture as the huge popularity of reggae in the 1970s demonstrated.

△ Teddy boys drinking in a milk bar, 1959.

The British and American magimix: 'The House of the Rising Sun' (1964)

The Tyneside group The Animals released this single in 1964. It tells the story of a life ruined by prostitution in New Orleans, yet despite the shocking theme of the song it shot to the top of the British charts. The tune may have originally been a seventeenth-century English folk song which was then adapted into an American ballad. A version had already been recorded by the American star Bob Dylan, but had not been a hit. The Animals' recording was influenced by many traditions including American black and folk music. It became an American number 1 and sold more than eight million copies across the world.

This mixing of American and British music was typical of the time, and reflects a more general cultural exchange. This was not new to the 1950s and 1960s; Hollywood films in the 1930s and American soldiers in the war also made an impact. Few would now accept Hoggart's interpretation of British teenagers losing their national identity and culture through the dominance of American commerce and media. Fewer still would deny that post-war Britain was partly shaped by the swinging hips of Elvis Presley, the power of US brands such as Levis and Coca-Cola and the image of the denim-clad, gum-chewing American youth.

> The first record I ever bought was 'Heartbreak Hotel' by Elvis, which came out in 1956. It really was an extraordinary new sound, so thrilling. My parents were appalled.
>
> (From a book of memories of the 1950s)

▇ To complete your study of Americanisation, remember to make notes as suggested on page 41 in order to sum up how far this aspect changed young people's lives.

Were young people corrupted by money?

Teenagers in the 1950s and 1960s had money to spend. Jobs were plentiful, wages were reasonable, and most young people lived at home, paying their parents a modest rent. Advertisers targeted the youth market, exploiting the growth of teen magazines and commercials on television and cinema. In 1959 Mark Abrams published the highly influential pamphlet *The Teenage Consumer* in which he concluded:

> There is distinct teenage spending for distinctive teenage ends in a distinctive teenage world.

Social commentators at the time, and historians later on, have seized on this as a key cause of the youth 'problem'. Without the need to provide for home or family, youths had affluence without responsibility. Young people were splashing out on expensive clothes, hanging out in local coffee bars and rushing to buy the latest pop releases from the record store. Money was used to challenge the adult world – motorbikes, loud pop albums, distinctive haircuts – all seemed to mock parental authority. With money in their pockets teenagers could focus on having fun; drink, drugs, bars and clubs were available to them. High **disposable incomes** were at the root of the new and troublesome phenomenon of youth rebellion.

But are these claims justified? A good starting point is to look more closely at Abrams' evidence.

disposable income
The money you have to spend once you have paid your essential bills

Abrams and the teenage consumer

Abrams and *The Teenage Consumer*

Whom did he study?
Working-class unmarried young people, mostly in London and the South East, aged 15 to 25.

Why did he write his report?
Abrams' research was commissioned by the London Press Exchange for businessmen intent on selling goods to the teenage market. They wanted a brief factual summary of young people's spending abilities and wishes. Abrams provided the round figures this audience required: total expenditure and average earnings.

When did he write it?
Abrams wrote it in 1959. This was a time of relatively buoyant employment (around 1.8 per cent unemployment) and rises in **real wages**, especially in London and the South East.

real wages
Earnings when the prices of goods and services have been taken into account

What did Abrams say?

He made several judgements about young people's spending:

- Real wages for young people had risen by 50 per cent compared to pre-war levels.

- Their disposable income had increased by as much as 100 per cent, representing an annual expenditure of around £830 million.

- Their spending was on particular goods such as records and record players (44 per cent), bikes and motorbikes (39 per cent) with clothes, soft drinks, the cinema and magazines also very popular. Fewer than 10 per cent drank alcohol once a week or more and most did not smoke.

What's missing from Abrams' study?

- A definitive nationwide picture of young people's incomes in the 1950s and 1960s. While Abrams suggested young men had as much as £5 a week to spend, studies in the 1960s in Brighton and Bury conclude their average spend was less than £2. It is likely there were important regional variations in spending as well as changes over time.

- An overview of all social classes and ages. Middle-class youngsters were mostly ignored as a majority were in education and not wage earners. Many working-class couples married young (the national average age was 22 for first marriage in 1959) and they were not the focus of Abrams' study.

- Evidence that young people's earning power was a new phenomenon of the post-war era. Numerous studies have pointed out that youth consumerism was an important feature of the inter-war economy.

A contradictory study

Pearl Jephcott conducted an academic survey into youth leisure habits using a random sample of 15–19-year-olds from three different working-class communities in Glasgow and West Lothian in 1964–66. Her findings contradicted Abrams' conclusions in some ways. Fewer than half of her sample had spending money of more than £3. She concluded that:

> The popular image of today's adolescent as having money to burn was certainly not true of the great majority of these Scottish boys and girls.

Few of these teenagers could afford motorbikes although most owned some kind of music player such as a transistor or record player. Their money was generally used for cigarettes, magazines and records and a surprisingly high proportion of their leisure time was spent at home, watching television with their families.

So was money the root of teenage trouble?

How strongly does the research support the view that spending power was a major cause of youth rebellion in the 1950s and 1960s? Certain new developments are undeniable such as growing sales of pop records, magazines and record players. Spending on clothes and haircuts to create a particular look was not a new phenomenon but more sophisticated media and the development of teen magazines spread these fashions more widely and more speedily. It was money that enabled young people to create and display their own identities. And these were emphatically different from the styles of their parents. But any connection between higher incomes and serious teenage misbehaviour is very hard to find.

> Only a generation ago teenagers wanted to be identified as adults as quickly as possible. Now teenagers spend heavily so that they will stay the way they are. This is the awful thing about it – the Peter Pan mentality. They won't accept the responsibility of growing up.
>
> (Mark Abrams, the *Daily Mirror*, 9 October 1963)

To complete your study of the influence of money, remember to make notes as suggested on page 41 in order to sum up how far this aspect changed young people's lives.

Were the young led astray by rock and roll?

Yes: The story of Mick Jagger

From his student days, Jagger was a rebel. He deliberately adopted a scruffy image, grew his hair long and dropped out of university. He became lead singer in the rhythm and blues band, the Rolling Stones, which quickly gained a reputation for rebellious and unorthodox music. In 1965 the hit single 'I Can't Get No Satisfaction' caused an outcry, with its sexually explicit and anti-commercial lyrics. In the same year Jagger and his fellow band members were convicted of 'insulting behaviour' for urinating in a petrol station forecourt. Drugs convictions followed, with a three-month sentence for possession of amphetamines in 1967. His song 'Street Fighting Man' was inspired by anti-war protests in 1968 and was banned by some radio stations which claimed it was subversive. One journalist commented that the Rolling Stones were boys 'whom any self-respecting mum would lock in the bathroom'. For the establishment, Jagger was a symbol of all that was wrong with the younger generation.

The case for the prosecution

- **Drugs:** Pop stars popularised drug use, initially cannabis and later amphetamines, such as LSD. The Beatles all publicly signed a letter supporting the legalisation of cannabis in 1967. Many leading singers were convicted of possession of drugs and lyrics in their hit songs made thinly veiled references to drug use, such as The Beatles' 'Lucy in the Sky with Diamonds' (LSD).

- **Sexual promiscuity:** Pop lyrics, suggestive dance moves and the personal behaviour of the stars encouraged more open and casual sexual behaviour. 'Elvis the Pelvis' was famous for his gyrating hips, a dancing style copied by British singers such as Cliff Richard. Leading stars like Jagger and Lennon were known for their numerous sexual liaisons.

- **Dropping out:** The hippie movement was boosted by the open adoption of Eastern mysticism and a bohemian lifestyle by some of the leading pop stars. Rejecting traditional institutions such as school and family, some young people adopted a carefree, irresponsible existence.

- **Rebelliousness:** The tone and beat of rock music itself seemed to challenge the softer dance music of the older generation. Rock and pop stars showed little deference to authority in their interviews and many espoused radical causes, such as opposition to the Vietnam War and support for the Campaign for Nuclear Disarmament.

- **Image:** Pop stars adopted 'looks' designed to appal the older generation and to make an impact with the young. At different times their appearance was scruffy, effeminate or offensive.

1956

Teddy boy audiences rioted in cinemas when 'Rock Around the Clock' was played as part of the film The Blackboard Jungle.

TEDDY BOYS RUN RIOT WHEN THE CLOCK STRIKES ONE!

1964

Lead singer of The Who, Pete Townshend, accidentally smashed his guitar during a performance in London. This proved so popular with the audience, the band made instrument breaking a regular feature of their show.

1965

The Kinks fought on stage during a concert in Cardiff. Their violent behaviour led to a ban in the USA.

1976

The punk band the Sex Pistols behaved outrageously during a BBC television interview, shocking the audience with frequent use of the 'f' word.

THE FILTH AND THE FURY

No: The story of Michael Fanshawe

Fanshawe was born in Kent, the son of a lecturer. He had a conventional middle-class upbringing, winning a place at grammar school and later at the prestigious London School of Economics. Music was a passion from an early age and he sang in the church choir. He did not complete his degree, choosing instead to devote himself to music. His band was successful and he became a leading pop star of the 1960s, one journalist describing him as 'unusually friendly and intelligent'. This was followed by a long and lucrative career in music and film. His fame brought him television interviews, magazine features and invitations to posh parties. In order to avoid tax on his massive fortune, Fanshawe has lived abroad since the 1970s. In 2003 he was knighted for his services to music.

The case for the defence

- **Romance more than sex:** The themes and lyrics of almost all the top-selling records of the 1960s were about teenage romance. In the 1960s harder edged music never rivalled the success of romantic songs.

- **Peace rather than protest:** The main protest songs of the era were on the general theme of peace and reconciliation, like Dylan's 'Blowin' in the Wind'. The anti-Vietnam protests, supported by many in the music world, did not challenge the British government which was not directly involved in the war. Few pop stars adopted a coherent radical political stance.

> The best-selling album of the 1960s was *The Sound of Music*.

- **Good role models:** Leading stars such as Cliff Richard, Cilla Black and Adam Faith came from modest working-class backgrounds yet built successful pop careers and acquired fortunes through talent and hard work. Their image and behaviour were innocuous.

- **Pride in Britain:** Youth culture and music had been dominated by the USA until the mid-1960s. The huge success of British bands restored pride in British creativity and innovation. British music proved a stimulus to films, fashion and magazines.

- **Image:** It was not until the mid-1960s that pop stars turned against smart suits and short hair. Even from this time on, most stars sought to add a touch of glamour to the stage rather than to provoke a reaction.

This band sold more records than the Rolling Stones in the 1960s. They were called The Shadows.

> John Lennon's hit song of 1969 was 'Give Peace a Chance'.

> The best-selling single of the decade was The Beatles' 'She Loves You'.

> The most successful British star in the 1960s was the clean-living Christian, Cliff Richard.

Summing up

You have probably guessed that Jagger and Fanshawe are the same person.

The apparent contradictions in his life story can partly be explained by the Stones' manager deliberately marketing his band as 'dangerous, dirty and degenerate', editing out the more 'respectable' aspects of their background and behaviour to mark them out as different from their rivals, The Beatles. This made them more appealing to their teenage market. When interviewed on television in 1967, 30 million viewers heard Jagger express respect for the older generation while also denying that drugs were in any way a 'crime against society'. There is no doubt that his behaviour became increasingly conventional as he grew older. So it is difficult to assess how bad this 'bad boy' of 1960s pop actually was. It is even more difficult to judge how much he influenced his fans. It seems likely, however, that, while thousands of boys experimented with Elvis quiffs in the 1950s or long hippie locks in the 1960s, only a minority were ever tempted to try LSD or heroin.

▷ Mick Jagger at the New Musical Express Poll Winners Concert, Wembley, 1966.

Were The Beatles a bad influence on the young?

Less than eighteen months after recording *Please Please Me*, The Beatles were the biggest rock act the world had ever seen … their hair, dress, music and even their accent copied by and influencing millions.

(J. Lawton, *1963 Five Hundred Days: History as Melodrama* (1992))

△ Hysterical teenage girls awaiting the arrival of The Beatles are held back by police.

The rise and rise of The Beatles in a decade

In 1965 the four Beatles were awarded MBEs. Before meeting the Queen, they huddled in the palace loos and shared a marijuana joint. The story was later denied yet it exemplifies the mix of respect and irresponsibility which runs throughout The Beatles' story. In some ways The Beatles can be seen as conventional conformists: most of them married rather than 'living in sin'. Lennon completed a lot of his work in his six-bedroomed house in Surrey. They made their money by telling us that 'All that you need is love'. They performed on the family-friendly Morecambe and Wise show and before the Queen in the Royal Variety Performance. While Lennon sometimes criticised politicians and the government, he never put forward an alternative political philosophy of his own and was dismissive of the idea of 'protest songs'. Their tone in interviews was playful rather than rude and by the late 1960s they were no longer regarded as a political or moral threat, having widened their appeal across British society.

The Beatles' career

1957	The teenage John Lennon and Paul McCartney met at a church fete in Liverpool.
1960–61	As a relatively unknown Liverpool band, they played at the Cavern Club.
1962	The group had modest success with their first release, 'Love Me Do', and were accepted by EMI record label. The Beatles released 'Twist and Shout' with its sexy beat and lyrics. Their new manager smartened up their image, took away their leather jackets and put them in grey suits.
1963	Their first TV appearance on *Thank Your Lucky Stars* was seen by 6 million viewers and the first major hit, 'Please Please Me', remained number 1 for 30 weeks. They began to win a mass following – the term 'Beatlemania' was coined by the *Daily Mirror*. *The Times* stated that Lennon and McCartney were the outstanding English composers of 1963.
1964	A highly successful tour of the USA. The film *A Hard Day's Night* was released, along with seven albums, four of which reached number 1 in the sales charts.
1965	The second film *Help!* was released. The Beatles were awarded MBEs by the Queen. A second US tour this year.
1966	The Beatles hold one last concert at Wembley then stop touring. They released two albums. John Lennon made a remark about the band being more popular than Jesus, which caused a negative backlash, particularly in the USA.
1967	*Sergeant Pepper's Lonely Hearts Club Band* was released and recognised as a major cultural breakthrough, making number 1 in the charts all over the world. Their third film *Magical Mystery Tour* was released to a mixed reception. The song 'Lucy in the Sky with Diamonds' was banned by the BBC for its supposed reference to the drug LSD.
1968	The band went to India and became interested in Eastern spiritualism. They created their own label, Apple Records, and released *The White Album*. Student protests inspired the Lennon/McCartney song 'Revolution'.
1969	The last performance in London. The final album, *Abbey Road*, was released. The band formally broke up in April 1970.

Yet at the time The Beatles had some serious critics. David Holbrook, a Cambridge academic, accused them of encouraging sexual interest in teenage girls and dulling the creativity of youth. The journalist Paul Johnson argued that Beatles' fans were 'the least fortunate of their generation, the dull, the idle, the failures'. A secondary school teacher confirmed their adverse influence on the young, stating that bright boys in her school wore Beatle haircuts, listened to transistor radios in the classroom and even walked round the school 'hand in hand'.

Modern commentators suggest that a more significant influence of The Beatles was the creation of a confident and independent youth culture and identity.

> They gave the kids something that they instinctively knew belonged to them and them alone. The Beatles were not owned by some recording company or some manager who cared only about the dollars. The Beatles belonged to themselves and, therefore, to their fans. Not only did the group sound original, they looked original, they approached the adult world with a certain originality and they were not, apparently, intimidated by that adult world. They exuded confidence. They made jokes with the press, laughed, made their music … and defied convention. They invented their own music. Sure, they played cover songs, but they also wrote their own. No Tin Pan Alley for this group. They had something to say and they said it. Thus began the rebellion, the revolution.
>
> (W. Fraser Sandercombe, *The Beatles: Press Reports 1961–1970* (2007))

Summing up: Were the young led astray by rock and roll?

Once again, simple generalisations are not possible here. There was no uniform teen culture of the 1950s and 1960s; young people's experiences varied hugely according to class, age, gender and location. A variety of kinds of music were followed, styles adopted and bars and clubs attended. David Fowler's research, for instance, has shown that in London only middle-class youth could afford to visit the new discotheques in the West End; working-class teenagers continued to meet in the same suburban dance halls their parents had known. Pop and rock gave young people new voices and new styles which set them apart from their parents. But this new musical culture was diverse, changeable and usually harmless.

■ To complete your study of the impact of rock and roll, remember to make notes as suggested on page 41 in order to sum up how far this aspect changed young people's lives.

Were the young led on by the far left?

> Arrogance, intolerance and puritanism are all to be expected from young rebels: they are the hallmarks of the tribe. Even their methods need cause little surprise, though the mindless shouting of slogans is always ugly and coming from people claiming to be intelligent, is contemptible and bad.
>
> (Letter to *The Times*, 12 June 1968)

militants
Extreme activists, prepared to use violence to pursue their cause

So wrote a Cambridge history professor in 1968 after student protesters interrupted a ceremony in the university senate house. He went on to argue that a vocal minority of **militants**, influenced by strident 'prophets' from outside Cambridge, had caused students to take this reprehensible action. Their demands for a say over their courses, over appointments and over teaching methods were dismissed as insane. His view was supported by a majority of the public, with only 15 per cent sympathising with student grievances according to one Gallup poll. At this time, after all, universities were still 'in loco parentis': young people became adult voting citizens only at the age of 21. Most universities imposed strict curfews on their students and rules about visits from the opposite sex.

There had been a massive expansion of higher education in the post-war years. Harold Wilson established eight new universities and 29 polytechnics in the years 1964–70 alone. One in ten young people attended university by the mid-1960s with government grants giving access to far more from poorer backgrounds than ever before. It was hard to understand how privileged young people, being paid by the state to learn, should have anything to protest about.

The facts about student protests

What proportion were protesting?

A poll at Warwick University in June 1968 found that only 7 per cent of students were active in politics and a survey at Cambridge in May 1968 showed that 21 per cent of the 302 students asked had taken part in a protest in the last year.

LSE
The London School of Economics

Even at one of the most radical institutions, the **LSE** in London, 60 per cent of students asked had taken no part in the protests at all.

What were they protesting about?

Protests against the Vietnam War were the most widely supported. Around 25 per cent of Sussex university students interviewed had joined in demonstrations against the war in 1968. The Vietnam Solidarity Campaign organised a protest in March 1968, attracting 25,000 young people who marched on the American embassy. There were some violent encounters with the police. This was followed by another mass demonstration in October, which mostly passed off peacefully. Half the October protesters were university students.

Opposition to nuclear weapons was also a popular cause. An estimated 90 per cent of CND membership were young people and many took part in the mass marches of the early 1960s.

Other student grievances concerned their own institutions. There were demands for fewer rules and regulations, student representation in governing bodies and more say over courses and teaching methods. A majority of students interviewed supported these issues although very few went as far as the students at the Hornsey College of Art whose demands included an end to all graded assessment and entry requirements.

Were student protests dominated by the left?

It was a common establishment view that student protests were whipped up by extreme left-wing radicals. The Director of the LSE blamed the sit-in of 1967 on 'a small group of about 50 left-wing students'. Tariq Ali, the Oxford student and leader of the Vietnam Solidarity Campaign, was certainly a committed Marxist and the Socialist journal, the *Black Dwarf*, was widely circulated on university campuses.

Yet the majority of British students were either moderate or apathetic. Even among those taking part in protests, only a small number were committed to radical politics: a survey of Liverpool University students in 1969 found that 28 per cent were Conservative (more than were Labour) and only 1 per cent identified with the far left. With regard to the two main socialist organisations in 1968 it is estimated that International Socialism had fewer than 500 members and the International Marxist Group only 40 members. When the far left did win more support, it appeared to be short lived. In the elections at the LSE in 1969, none of the militant candidates was elected.

Furthermore, student support for radical causes did not mean they endorsed the more extreme views of the Marxists. More than 40 per cent of those Vietnam protesters wanted a peaceful settlement of the war rather than a Vietnamese victory over 'American imperialism'. And only 5 per cent of Cambridge and Sussex university students interviewed in 1968 approved of violence in demonstrations.

What did British students get up to?

January 1967	A university porter died at a student protest meeting at the LSE. This was followed by a nine-day sit-in and 1000 demonstrators marching through London. More than half of students refused to attend lectures during the dispute.
January 1969	LSE forced to close for a month due to student sit-ins.
May 1968	200–300 students at the University of Hull organised a sit-in against their final examinations. It lasted for two days. There were similar sit-ins at various universities including Essex and Leeds. At Essex more than 1000 students protested at the banning of a student union leader.

The international perspective

In Europe and the USA there were very serious outbreaks of youth protest. In France in 1968 the universities of the Sorbonne and Nanterre were occupied by 30,000 students for over a month. Five students were killed in street fighting with the police and 600 students arrested on a single day. Students allied with striking workers to attack the government on a number of issues. A general strike and demonstration in May was supported by 1 million people. In America, up to 10,000 students took part in the 'Freedom of Speech Movement' at the University of California.

British students showed little support for international youth rebellion. A rally planned to show solidarity with the French protesters attracted low numbers.

So were students in the 1960s a bunch of dangerous lefties?

There's no doubt that many students at this time embraced left-wing politics and some became Marxists. Coming up to university in London for the first time, one student commented that she came:

> ... straight from a girls' convent school in Wiltshire to revolutionary politics at **SOAS** where membership of the Labour Party wasn't considered to be left-wing enough.

SOAS
School of Oriental and African Studies, part of the University of London

A survey of the marchers at Grosvenor Square showed that 68 per cent were against 'capitalism in general'. Yet this vague adoption of radical views never developed into a more coherent movement. In France there was collaboration with trade unionists and working-class activists. In the USA student protests embraced civil rights. In the UK the student movement was more diverse and incoherent. Lots of students went on marches against the Vietnam War or joined in sit-ins, demanding more say over university management. But then they went back to writing their essays.

So what can be concluded about the influence of left-wing politics? In social history, as we have seen, it is often very difficult to measure the impact of one factor on social behaviour and compare it with others. In this case student radicalism varied hugely over time and place and took a range of forms so it is another case of drawing several qualified conclusions rather than making one clear judgement:

- Most student protesters were not members of extreme left-wing groups nor did they hold a coherent set of socialist views.

- Large numbers of British students adopted political campaigns such as CND and anti-Vietnam protests without becoming committed socialists.

- While some student leaders were militants, they failed to hold on to any sustained support.

- In some universities such as the LSE, militants took the lead in protests but in others, such as Liverpool, they had minimal influence.

- Unlike protests abroad, student challenges to authority in Britain were mostly legal and short-lived.

■ To complete your study of far-left politics, remember to make notes as suggested on page 41 in order to sum up how far this aspect changed young people's lives.

Review: Why did teenagers' lives seem to be changing?

There was a strong perception, particularly in the older generation, that young people's lives dramatically changed at this time. But can this view be substantiated or did it just 'seem' to be the case?

Perception	Reality
There was a sharp rise in juvenile crime such as football hooliganism.	There was a slight rise in youth crime in the 1950s and 1960s with a levelling off in the 1970s. More than two-thirds of arrests for football hooliganism in the 1970s were for 'insulting words' or 'threatening behaviour' rather than acts of violence. As in the past, most crime was committed by 15–21-year-olds and the most common offences were theft, burglary and criminal damage. Gang culture and petty theft continued to be well-established features of life in many working-class communities.
Drugs and drink became a much more serious problem.	There was, and always had been, a strong link between drink and crime. Arrests for drunkenness became slightly more common and there is some evidence that drinking was starting at an earlier age. There was a sharp rise in convictions for drug use, particularly marijuana. In 1960 only 235 people were found guilty of possession compared to more than 11,000 in 1973. The vast majority of cases involved soft not hard drugs. According to the historian Paul Addison, the spread of drug use was 'the most important and enduring consequence of 1960s youth culture'.
Young people became much more rebellious.	Young people had certainly played a part in riots, football violence and in unemployment marches before 1945. What was new in the 1960s were larger scale student protests against the Vietnam War and for CND. This was not accompanied by any measurable decline in respect for parents or the law.

Surveys of British youth show that they were generally a pretty well-behaved and conservative bunch. In the longer term British students were more concerned about passing their exams than showing solidarity with international socialism. Pop stars were not a consistent radical force; John Lennon did not join in the anti- Vietnam protests in Britain nor did he support lowering the voting age to eighteen. Working-class subcultures lacked stamina, fading away or softened by commercialisation. By their mid-twenties, the mods and rockers who had terrorised the seaside resorts in their teens were mostly married and had settled down. They were then more likely to spend their hard-earned cash on renting a television and buying a new bathmat than on jackets, knives or boots.

Misguided views of what young people were like were largely created by newspapers and television. A Bradford University study of newspaper reporting of young people in 1979 concluded that the press created an image of a typical adolescent as:

> ... a sporting youngster, criminally inclined, likely to be murdered or injured in an accident.

In an era increasingly dominated by the mass media, this image of youth was likely to stick. And throughout time, as we have seen, the older generation has happily latched on to a belief that their children are worse behaved than they were.

Summing up: What caused young people's lives to change?

A view based on sociological theory

In the 1970s, the left-wing founders of the Centre for Cultural Studies at Birmingham, Stuart Hall and Richard Hoggart, stressed the importance of social and economic change in causing youth rebellion. The breaking up of working-class communities, they have argued, caused urban youngsters to seek new identities and challenge authority. They attached great significance to working-class resistance and subcultures. Rejections of authority such as Teddy boys ripping up cinema seats, football violence by skinheads and hippies dropping out were all interpreted as ways young people asserted their political identity. Yet their sociological and Marxist perspectives on the topic have made their writings controversial. The modern historian, David Fowler, has commented:

> Much of this research is so devoid of serious scholarly analysis as not to merit detailed engagement with.

A view based on contemporary research

In the mid-1960s, when Pearl Jephcott asked working-class teenagers why fights developed they provided a more mundane reason – boredom:

> They gave the impression that much, perhaps most, of the fights had no more serious motive than to try to liven things up a bit. Of Drumchapel [a large, post-war housing estate in Glasgow with few amenities], they said that the place was dead, and that after the weekend, which took most of their money, they had absolutely nothing to do. Compared with the only too well-known routines of home, job and after-work hours, a fight at least offered a possibility of the unfamiliar.

Neither academic theory nor contemporary evidence can provide a watertight explanation of changes in young people's behaviour. Sociological theories have been strongly challenged by historians requiring more concrete evidence to support them. As for Jephcott's study, the dangers of generalising from one sample or accepting teenage explanations at face value are very clear. Yet this study is a useful reminder that youth rebellion could be spontaneous and opportunistic rather than the result of longer term social or cultural trends.

The causes of post-war youth rebellion, such as it was, are clearly highly contentious. Most would now accept that a mixture of reasons lay behind the significant, if not dramatic, challenges to authority. Even with 'serious scholarly analysis' it is very hard to prove which influences had most weight. With these thoughts in mind, here are some suggested overall conclusions:

- Popular music provided a common language and culture which often eroded barriers of class and region.

- University education and a prosperous job market assisted the creation of new youth styles, tastes and political engagement.

- The mass media and commerce helped to spread and unify youth trends, whether it was Beatlemania or support for CND.

- Post-war teens got into trouble, just like their predecessors. The way their troubles were perceived and the way they developed were moulded largely by the evolving economy and society in which they lived.

Reach your own conclusions on the subject: Why did teenagers' lives seem to be changing?

1 Bring together the notes you have made after each section, when you considered:

   a the impact of each influence

   b why some people saw this impact as i) positive ii) negative

   c how far teenage lives were really changed by each influence.

2 Explain the ways in which these influences worked together, for instance, how teenage spending power affected their adoption of subcultures and their involvement in rock and roll.

3 Finally, consider why many people thought that teenagers' lives were changing more than they actually were, using the final section of this chapter.

A closer look at photographs

One of the great benefits of studying modern Britain is the sheer range of photographs available as evidence – a quick action shot in a war zone, a family snapshot or a celebrity portrait – just to name a few. The technology used, the particular photographer and the context and purpose of the photo will influence the nature of the image, so when using photographs you need to find out as much about their origins as possible. Remember that photos can be edited, touched up and coloured and that manipulation of photographs is as old as the art of photography itself.

The rich and famous have always protected their image – Elizabeth I strictly controlled her own portraits in the sixteenth century so that, even in old age, her image still looked young. In the 1960s the Beatles were equally concerned about how they presented themselves to the public, although they had to compromise with record companies and managers. Photos of the band were highly valued; being used for posters, magazines and album covers, which all played a major role in marketing the Beatles' brand and in making money from it.

Case study one: The Beatles in 1963

The photo

This photograph (right) is a group studio portrait. It is clearly posed and taken by a professional photographer in his studio. This means that great care will have been taken over dress, make-up and hairstyles, and this shot will probably have been selected from many taken in one session. The photographer will also have set up the lighting and background to achieve the desired impression.

The context

When manager Brian Epstein agreed to take on the Beatles in 1962, he had insisted that they clean up their look. The leather jackets and uncropped hair were replaced with tailored suits and neat 'moptop' hairstyles. They had released their first number 1 hit 'Please Please Me' in the spring of 1963 and Beatlemania was just taking off. At this time their albums were still filled with the traditional love songs favoured by their teen admirers, such as 'Love Me Do'.

By the autumn of 1963, the Beatles were also winning broader approval. They appeared at the Royal Variety performance and were applauded by the Queen Mother and a respectable middle-aged audience, as well as attracting a television audience of 26 million. An article in the *Daily Mirror* complimented them on their moptop hairstyles which were washed and 'superclean' and their fan base which ranged from 'Wapping to Windsor' and aged 'seven to seventy'. In December 1963, even the music critic of the highbrow *Times* newspaper was singing their praises.

What does this photo tell us?

In some ways this image is a traditional pop band photo, similar to the plush black and white images of stars such as Presley which were common at the time. The band look smart and well groomed and they are clearly smiling for the camera. They are presented as a team; in identical, tailored suits, not as individuals. It's a picture that would please both their teen fans and their more disapproving parents and reflects the broad appeal they had achieved by the autumn of 1963. Yet the Beatles, even at this stage, were establishing their own particular style. The moptop hairstyles contrasted with the short back and sides or Teddy boy quiffs that were common at the time and in 1963 schoolboys were being sent home for sporting this unconventional look. The distinctive collarless suits were inspired by Pierre Cardin's latest designs. Brian Epstein had chosen these grey suits, with black piping, to create a younger and less severe image. This picture tells us how the band, their backers and their manager wanted to present them in 1963: stylish young men one's daughters could date.

Case study two : The Beatles in 1967

reflected these new ideas. In a later interview, McCartney recalled their feelings at the time:

> We were fed up with being the Beatles. We really hated that f——g four little moptop boys approach. We were not boys, we were men. It was all gone, all that boy shit, all that screaming, we didn't want any more, plus, we'd now got turned on to pot and thought of ourselves as artists rather than just performers…

The photo

For the launch of the Beatles' eagerly awaited new album, *Sergeant Pepper's Lonely Hearts Club Band*, Brian Epstein hosted a promotional party at his house in London. A small group of reporters and press photographers were invited to hear the album in advance and to take pictures of the band as they relaxed in their manager's home (see above). Naturally the resulting images were much more casual and less staged than the studio portrait taken in 1963. Nevertheless, there was little accidental or haphazard about how the Beatles presented themselves on this occasion as the party was deliberately set up as a photo opportunity for the press.

The context

The summer of 1967 was nicknamed the 'summer of love' because it was associated with the rise of the hippie movement, flower power and anti-Vietnam protests.

By 1967 the Beatles had abandoned their clean-cut boy band image and were presenting themselves as creative and independent musical artists. Live performances had been abandoned and the band spent time in the recording studio instead. They were now rich, well established and independent. Their reputation, previously contrasted favourably with the Rolling Stones, was no longer so pure, with public acknowledgements of the use of the drug LSD. In 1967 the Beatles were showing an interest in Eastern religion and embracing new avant garde ideas such as electronic music and psychedelic art. By this time they had the means, the money, and the motivation to produce an album that

What does this photo tell us ?

This photo contrasts strongly with the clean-cut, smiley team image of 1963. The four stand together closely arm in arm, with longer hair and moustaches: their faces a mix of indifference, challenge and boredom. Their clothes demonstrate their individuality, with Ringo in a conventional suit and the others in an eclectic mix of formal jackets and frilly dress shirts. Lennon shows his humour by wearing a sporran to keep his keys and cigarettes handy, he claims, while George wears a badge from the New York Workshop of Non-Violence, evidence of his commitment to Eastern pacifism. The photo confirms that the band were now more in control of their own image rather than being moulded by managers and record companies or worried by public disapproval. In less than a year their manager would be dead and they would have set up their own business to manage their affairs. This picture tells us how the Beatles wished to appear just before the release of their most innovative album: as four creative personalities, comfortable with their own beliefs and styles.

This study shows that even celebrity photographs can vary greatly according to their context and purpose. Early in their career the Beatles conformed to the traditional look that sold records and pleased commercial record companies. Later, as a world-famous band, they could present themselves more or less as they wished. Sadly, it is often hard to find information about the origins of photographs, with many books telling you little apart from the subject and the date. Yet the more you can discover about the nature and purpose of these images, the more valuable the pictures become as evidence.

4 Was sex shaken up in the 1960s?

Introduction

> I feel I must protest at the proposed institution of a 'sex clinic' in Sheffield. The doctors say that their desire is to prevent the birth of unwanted children, but surely they must realise that by the widespread issue of contraceptives they are removing the only natural barrier to illicit sex – the fear of conception – and encouraging a moral delinquency which is already woefully out of hand.

'Annus Mirablis' by Philip Larkin

Sexual intercourse began

In nineteen sixty-three

(Which was rather late for me) –

Between the end of the *Chatterley* ban

And The Beatles' first **LP**.

LP
Short for 'long playing', a type of vinyl record consisting of numerous tracks

See Chapter 5 for how Penguin's publication of D.H. Lawrence's book *Lady Chatterley's Lover* caused a major upset in 1960.

This letter was published in the *Sheffield Star* in September 1966, criticising the setting up of a clinic that offered contraceptive advice to unmarried women. One of the first of its kind outside London, the clinic was established by two female doctors who deliberately catered for young people. It was a project without state support or funds – all the staff worked for nothing in the first year and the premises were secured with a £500 loan from a well wisher. Both women faced widespread condemnation, especially from the Churches. One of these women was my mother.

This is the story people usually tell of the 'swinging sixties'. Traditionally it's a decade when the rebellious young overturned the conservative morals of their parents. Before this 'revolution' it is often said that there was 'no sex before marriage', couples stayed together, with the man in charge of the household. Homosexuality was illegal. Afterwards there was sexual freedom, easy divorce, legal abortion and tolerance of homosexuality. Women now raced out to work and the homely traditions of women 'having tea on the table when dad gets in' seemed lost forever. In this decade, it used to be thought, attitudes to sex and to the equality of the sexes were severely shaken up.

Yet it is not as simple as this. The opponent of the sex clinic in the letter above described himself as a 'young person and a university student' and he was supported by sixth formers calling for 'self control not birth control'. In response, the clinic was defended by letters from the older generation. Sex certainly shook up society in the 1960s but it was not a simple story of young versus old. Some historians have argued that the real upset happened in the 1970s while others suggest that the changes were gradual and on-going; more evolutionary than revolutionary. Historians of women's and gay history have argued that little progress with equality and justice was made at all. Evidence on these issues is partial, patchy and sometimes prejudiced. Your challenge, to assess the nature and extent of social change, is therefore a difficult one.

■ **Enquiry Focus:** Was sex shaken up in the 1960s?

The focus of this enquiry is the extent to which attitudes and behaviour in matters of sex, gender and sexuality really did change in British society in the post-war years and in particular whether the 1960s was the decade when sex was shaken up.

It requires consideration of the following key issues:

1 The nature and extent of changes in sexual attitudes and behaviour, including legal changes

2 The impact of new forms of birth control

3 Changing views of women's employment

4 Women's liberation

5 Evolving attitudes to homosexuality.

As you work your way through this chapter, annotate your version of the 'shockometer' below, marking where you judge each of topics 1–5 should be placed on it.

To reach your judgement on where each topic should go on the 'shockometer' first make notes:

a explaining attitudes *before* the 1960s and whether change was taking place

b identifying the key changes in the 1960s and how great they seemed to be at the time

c on the extent of further changes after the 1960s.

Then use your notes on a–c to judge where each of 1–5 should go on the 'shockometer'.

Was sex being shaken up in the 1960s?

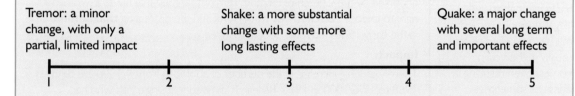

Tremor: a minor change, with only a partial, limited impact

Shake: a more substantial change with some more long lasting effects

Quake: a major change with several long term and important effects

1   2   3   4   5

Shakes and quakes in sexual attitudes and behaviour: was there a 'seismic shift' in the 1960s?

1960s Britain witnessed a seismic shift in attitudes towards sex and sexuality. The contraceptive pill made casual sex easier and safer. The 1957 Wolfenden Report recommended the decriminalisation of homosexuality, finally legalised in 1967, and abortion and divorce were made easier. All this led to the idea of a 'permissive society'.

(From the Tate Britain website)

The reputation of the 'sexy sixties' is endorsed in this blurb for an exhibition of 1960s art in 2004. But how far is this reputation deserved? We'll begin with changes in the law as this decade was noted for important new legislation, which may indicate significant shifts in public attitudes to sexual matters.

Changes in the law: spotlight on two shaky moments

backstreet abortions
Illegal abortions carried out by unqualified people, usually in their own homes, often resulting in illness or sometimes death for the woman

thalidomide
A drug given to pregnant women to ease morning sickness in the years 1958–61. Unfortunately it was later found to have caused severe birth defects in babies

promiscuous
Having casual sexual relations with many different partners

Abortion Act 1967

Abortion was legalised in the first 28 weeks of pregnancy provided two doctors confirmed it was necessary on medical or psychological grounds. Four previous attempts to change the law on abortion had failed, as it was such a divisive issue and strongly opposed by the Catholic Church. One 1965 survey, however, showed that 70 per cent of the public supported reform and it was also endorsed by the Church of England. Feminists argued that it was a 'woman's right to choose'. **Backstreet abortions** and the distressing **thalidomide** case in the early 1960s led most people to agree.

Impact

There was a big increase in the number of abortions from 4/1000 live births in 1968 to 17.6/1000 in 1975. Research showed that single girls who had abortions were more likely to be inexperienced than **promiscuous**, so there was little evidence that the new law was encouraging casual sex. Opposition to legal abortion remained strong with one professor shocking his audiences with a bottle of foetuses when speaking on the issue. Attempts to repeal the Act failed nevertheless.

In the 1970s and 1980s, access to abortion remained difficult for many women, despite the new law. Most doctors were male and some disapproved of abortion, making it difficult to win consent from two doctors in some areas of the country. Feminists stated that the 1967 Act still gave men unacceptable power over women. By the twenty-first century it was estimated that one in four women had had an abortion during their lifetime, suggesting the practice had become widespread and more generally accepted.

Divorce Reform Act 1969

Previously divorce had been based on proving guilt or fault in one partner, leading some couples to set up fake examples of adultery or to gather or pay for evidence themselves, in order to end their marriages. The new law enabled marriages to be dissolved on the grounds of 'irretrievable breakdown' or a seven-year separation. The Anglican and Methodist Churches approved the new 'no fault' divorces as did a majority of the public. But there was some concern that wives and children would suffer when marriages ended after the desertion of the man who then had no obligation to care for his family. Baroness Summerskill, a leading Labour politician and feminist, called the new law a 'Casanova's Charter' for this reason.

Impact

The divorce rate rose sharply. In 1965 there were 2.8 divorces/1000 married adults. By 1976 this had risen to 9.6 and five years later it reached 12, giving Britain one of the highest divorce rates in Europe. Women were recognised as equal partners in marriage and a further law, in 1970, required women's work inside and outside the home to be taken into account in all divorce settlements.

Women were more likely to suffer financially after divorce than men. Despite their legal rights to property and maintenance, women heading single-parent households had lower incomes than their ex-husbands. Widespread social disapproval of divorce persisted, more often directed at women than men.

The divorce rate reached a peak in 1995 with a third of marriages ending in divorce within fifteen years. By this time divorce had become much more socially acceptable. Since an important test case in 1996, the rights of women who have been home-based have been legally recognised and divorce settlements have helped women to live independently after separation.

Changes in public attitudes

While legal changes are clear-cut – they happen or they don't – there is a lot of controversy about how far sexual attitudes and behaviour genuinely changed in the 1960s and the idea of a 'sexual revolution' is strongly contested.

It is tempting to compare the sexual habits of the 1960s with those of the twenty-first century and reach the conclusion that the older generations were naively well behaved.

'Today's women have three times more sex than their mothers' declared a *Daily Mail* headline in March 2010, comparing numbers of sexual partners in the 1960s to today. But this modern comparison is neither helpful nor accurate, assuming as it does that more partners means more sex. The fuzzy black and white televisions of the 1960s would not impress in our current high-tech world, yet they transformed British homes all the same. Judgements about the 1960s need to be made in terms of what happened before and after.

'If only he'd made love to me instead of using me like a chamber pot.'
(Anonymous respondent to a survey in 1949)

▽ **Table 4.1:** Births outside marriage (% of total births) 1951–81 (from OPCS)

	1951	1961	1971	1981
Births outside marriage (UK)	5.0	5.8	8.4	12.8

▽ **Table 4.2:** Divorce in England and Wales 1951–81 (from OPCS)

	1951	1961	1971	1981
Number divorcing (per 1000 married people)	2.6	2.1	6.0	11.9

▽ **Table 4.3:** UK marriage rates 1951–81 (from OPCS)

	1950	1960	1970	1980
Marriages per 1000 unmarried men	58	62	81	60

▽ **Table 4.4:** Key findings of Michael Schofield's research 1965–73 (see also page 91)

Sexual Behaviour of Young People (Schofield, 1965)	By the age of 16, 14% of boys and 5% of girls were sexually experienced.
	By the age of 18, 34% of boys and 17% of girls were sexually experienced.
Sexual Behaviour of Young Adults (Schofield, 1973) (a follow-up of the same interviewees)	At aged 21, 75% of men and 71% of women were sexually experienced.
	40% had either no experience on their wedding day or only experience with their spouse-to-be.

The conclusion must be that sexual intercourse before marriage is quite common and acceptable among young people, although it does not appear to start quite as early as some people think or fear. When these young people do seek sexual experience, in the majority of cases it is with someone they know very well, and it is often with someone they love and will marry.

(Schofield, p. 162)

▽ **Table 4.5:** Geoffrey Gorer survey *Sex and Marriage in England Today* (1969)

One-quarter of male respondents and two-thirds of females were virgins on their wedding day. 20% of men and 25% of women were married to the person they had first had intercourse with.

(Hall, p. 173)

Above is a range of statistical evidence for you to consider. Table 4.1 confirms a significant rise in the number of illegitimate births although this is continuing a trend started in the 1950s. The divorce rate (Table 4.2) did rise, but this may be largely due to a liberalisation in the law, making it much easier to end marriages. The most significant change in the 1960s was the notable rise in the marriage rate (Table 4.3), suggesting traditional values were enduring. The research evidence in Tables 4.4 and 4.5 does not suggest a huge rise in casual sex in the 1960s, more a continuing belief that it should only take place in the context of a long-term relationship. Therefore the statistics suggest that the 1960s was a time of significant change but these changes were gradual and ongoing rather than revolutionary.

Were the 'swinging sixties' the time of most change?

So far we've looked at what was happening in the 1960s but how much change had been happening before this – and how much took place afterwards? It's only by examining the degree of change before and after that we can assess the importance of the 1960s.

Flirty forties and fifties?

This was apparently a time of careful conservatism:

- People were marrying younger, more often and staying together longer. This was the heyday of marriage and nuclear families.
- Nice girls were expected to say 'No' until they had a ring on their finger but bridegrooms were not expected to be virgins.
- Women were expected to play a passive role in sex and contraception. One survey found a third of women rarely enjoyed sex.
- Pre-marital sex was frowned on; a British Medical Association booklet that appeared to be giving advice to unmarried couples caused an outcry in 1959 and had to be withdrawn.
- Attitudes were still strict: a Royal Commission decided against easier divorce and a majority of the public thought homosexuality was sinful.
- In working-class communities particularly, the man was regarded as the main breadwinner and master of the home.

but
- Sex was talked about more openly; a best-selling book of 1959 urged women to overcome the problem of frigidity.
- Attitudes were beginning to change: a 1956 *Daily Mirror* survey showed that 50 per cent of readers agreed with abortion on request.
- Rates of illegitimacy and divorce started to rise in the 1950s.
- Young men and women, especially in the cities, were becoming more liberal and experimental in sexual matters.

Saucy seventies and eighties?

These appear to be decades of even more major change:

- More liberal laws on divorce, abortion and homosexuality were passed in the late 1960s, only making an impact in these decades.
- The pill only became easily obtainable for all from 1974 when it was provided on the NHS, free of charge, and from GPs.

- Illegitimacy and rates of teenage pregnancy increased significantly.

- The rate of marriage declined from 1972 at the same time that more unmarried couples decided to live together. By the early 1990s less than 1 per cent of first intercourse took place within marriage.

- The first illustrated paperback sex guide, Alex Comfort's *Joy of Sex*, which was published in 1972, became an instant bestseller.

- Gay and feminist organisations became well established and active in these years.

but

- Traditional attitudes to sex and relationships remained strong. A British Social Attitudes survey of 1987 revealed that a quarter of people interviewed thought that pre-marital sex was wrong and nearly three-quarters condemned homosexual relations. Polls in the 1990s showed that most people were still seeking one partner for life and valued sexual fidelity.

- Although marriage happened later, it continued to be popular and those who divorced were not put off marrying again.

> The freedom that women were supposed to have found in the 1960s largely boiled down to easy contraception and abortion; things to make life easier for men, in fact.
>
> (Julie Burchill)

Feminists such as Julie Burchill have argued that the advances of the 1960s did little to help women's rights.

Most writers of sex manuals up until 1972 were middle-aged men with some scientific or medical background. A good proportion had strong religious convictions and most promoted traditional views of marriage and sex. Many writers made the assumption that women should play a passive role, such as the best-selling *Power of Sexual Surrender* (1958), which claimed that women should happily embrace the sexual demands of their husbands while accepting their primary role in life as wife and mother.

Then, in 1972, along came Alex Comfort's *Joy of Sex*. The title said it all – this was an illustrated and detailed guide which promoted the pleasure of sex for its own sake. Comfort described it as 'the first sexually explicit book for the coffee table'. An instant bestseller, for many the book brought the sexual revolution into ordinary homes.

It is now time to review whether sex was shaken up in the 1960s, using the information on changes in the law and social attitudes given above.

1 Consider the following questions and then use them to make your judgement on the 'shockometer'.

   a How much had sexual attitudes and behaviour begun changing before the 1960s?

   b What were the key changes in sexual attitudes and behaviour in the 1960s and how great did they seem to be at the time? (Remember to include changes in the law.)

   c Were the changes in sexual attitudes and behaviour even greater after the 1960s?

2 Use your notes on a–c to decide where you judge the topic 'Sexual attitudes and behaviour' should go on the 'shockometer'.

Did the pill cause a 'sexplosion' in the 1960s?

Personal story

My mother was appalled to discover that she was expecting me in the autumn of 1958. Who could blame her? She was only 31 yet had already had six children and a miscarriage in eight years. I was proof that neither a **diaphragm** nor a condom was as reliable as hoped. After I was born she went to great lengths to organise **sterilisation**, still disapproved of by many doctors. If her married life had started ten years later, the pill would have helped my parents to limit their family to two or three and I would not have put in an appearance at all.

diaphragm
An inter-uterine device (IUD), a form of contraception that could be inserted into the uterus

sterilisation
An operation to make women infertile, often involving closing the fallopian tubes.

So did the development of the contraceptive pill revolutionise contraception and sexual behaviour in the 1960s? The following two quotations suggest that it did.

Gavin Hodge, a hairdresser, comments in a book of memories of the 1960s:

There were two phases to the 1960s: pre-pill and post-pill. My sister, who was growing up in the late 1950s, didn't have half the freedom: if you got into trouble back then, you had to get married or you ended up down a **back street** with a coathanger. Then the pill came along – it gave women the freedom to be the equal of their boyfriends. There was a lot of moral debate at the time but, as far as I could gather, most girls couldn't care less about that: they just wanted to get their hands on it. We smoked a bit of dope, did a bit of acid, but the major drug of the 1960s was the pill.

back street
This is a reference to backstreet abortions (see page 68). These were carried out by local 'experts' who charged large sums of money to end pregnancies unofficially and illegally. They often had no medical training and the procedures often caused illness and sometimes death

Brian Masters is the author of *Swinging Sixties*, which was published in 1985. He was a young man in the 1960s who later went on to work as a writer and biographer.

People copulated on the slightest pretext after an acquaintance of some minutes. Sexual partners were snapped up and discarded without ceremony, provided that they had the newly available contraceptive pill in their pocket or handbag.

Swinging sixties + the Pill = sexual revolution

The evidence for a 1960s sexual revolution based on the pill seems overwhelming. It has been acclaimed as the biggest medical advance of the twentieth century and there is no doubt that it brought massive changes to sexual relationships. In particular:

- It gave women control over their own fertility. Research by Kate Fisher has shown that up until the 1950s men were primarily in charge of contraception. The pill reversed these roles.
- It separated contraception from the sexual act. This made sex more spontaneous and birth control far more convenient. Condoms and IUDs were never very popular because they required preparation before sex could take place.
- It raised expectations of contraception as the pill was far more reliable than any previous methods. This greatly reduced the risk of unwanted pregnancy. For women this could be liberating; it allowed them to pursue careers and become more financially independent. For men, it made it easier to pressurise girls to have sex and to avoid any long-term commitment.
- It changed the lives of single women. Before the pill, many teenage brides were pregnant, the resultant marriage forced on the couple to preserve the girl's reputation. Single motherhood was simply not an option and backstreet abortions were expensive and risky.
- It became the major form of contraception for most British women. A 1985 survey revealed that only 5 per cent of women aged 16–29 had never used it.

Yet many modern historians challenge this view of a very rapid transformation. The two quotations on page 73 were noticeably from city-dwelling men and so are unlikely to represent the views of the majority. There is strong evidence that the real impact of the pill was not so great:

- In the 1960s the most popular form of birth control remained the condom. These were readily available; from 1965 they could be bought at Boots, the High Street chemists. Even by 1969 only 15 per cent of married women under 45 were using the pill. It was not until 1974 that it was available free to all women through the NHS and not until 1975 that GPs routinely prescribed it.
- At first the pill was mainly used by better educated, young and middle-class women such as university students.
- Many working-class women did not wish to take over responsibility for birth control from men. Men liked controlling fertility and many women still wanted to play a more passive and more 'feminine' role in the sexual relationship.
- It is unlikely the pill led directly to increased sexual promiscuity. Rising rates of pre-marital sex predate the widespread availability of the pill. Added to that, surveys suggest that promiscuity and teenage pregnancies were far more prevalent among those not aware of birth control.

It took a while for some women to understand how to use the pill. One woman put it in her ear before having sex!

The problems of contradictory evidence

So what was sex and birth control in the 1960s really like? An exciting time of liberation and revolt as memoirs and anecdotes might suggest? Or cautious continuation of post-war trends as modern researchers assert? And why are views so different?

There can be no simple answer but here are some possible explanations to mull over. Information about sexual attitudes and behaviour is very limited and sometimes unreliable. People were inhibited about talking about their intimate lives and it is also probable that what they said in surveys differed from their private actions. This was particularly true of working-class couples and rural communities. Furthermore, published memoirs, diaries and letters of this era are dominated by those who set the trends and fashions such as models, pop stars and writers and by the educated middle class; all were much more radical in their views and behaviour than most of the public.

Finally, in his book *Sixties Britain: Culture, Society and Politics*, Mark Donnelly has shown how modern views of the 1960s are often shaped by:

- **Hindsight** Later values and attitudes colour our view of the decade. In the late 1960s, for instance, condoms remained the main method of contraception. It is only when looking back that the arrival of the pill seems so significant.

- **Modern-day attitudes** In the twenty-first century sexual attitudes and behaviour are much more relaxed and it is tempting to highlight the steps towards this more liberal future when studying the past. This encourages stereotypical judgements, such as the view that most young people were breaking the traditional sexual rules when most were actually quite restrained.

- **Political viewpoints** Those on the right tend to seize evidence of family breakdown and look back nostalgically on previous decades as times of old-fashioned family values. Examples from the 1960s are used as warnings of the dangers of too much moral laxity as a lesson for modern times. Those on the left highlight the new sexual freedoms gained by women and young people. They see the 1960s as a time when the authority of the conservative elites was rightly challenged. Therefore both those on the left and the right tend to emphasise the extent of change rather than continuity.

Assessing the impact of the pill is very tricky as these pages show.
1 Consider the questions below to help you to decide where to place the 'Impact of the pill' on the 'shockometer'.
  a How far did the pill change sexual behaviour? Think about which groups of people were most or least affected by this new form of contraception.
  b Was it in the 1960s that the pill had its greatest impact? Assess the evidence that it was not until the 1970s and 1980s that the pill made a major difference to sexual behaviour.
2 Use your notes on a–b to decide where you judge the topic 'The impact of the pill' should go on the 'shockometer'.

Was women's work in a whirl?

What were women doing in the 1960s and 1970s?

My mum was working part time as a GP, helping to run a birth control clinic and being mother to six children.

Bella Keyzer was reluctantly working on the trams as her gender barred her from the wartime welding job on the shipyards she had loved. She was finally able to take this up again in 1975 when the law on sex discrimination was changed.

Margery Hurst was running the biggest secretarial agency in the world. Abandoned with a small baby by her husband after the war, she set up her own business, Brook Street, providing much needed typists for London firms.

Sandie Shaw was becoming a pop idol, known for singing in bare feet and setting fashion trends. On her marriage in 1968 she signed away her fortune to her husband and recovered little of her money on her divorce two years later.

Yvonne Pope had a job as an air traffic controller, working towards her ambition to become a pilot for a major airline. She achieved this in 1975.

May Hobbs was working night shifts, cleaning offices in London. Pay and conditions were so poor she struggled to support her family and pay the rent. She set up a union and organised a cleaners' strike in 1972.

Ravinder Randhawa, daughter of an immigrant factory worker and cleaner, fulfilled her parents' dreams by graduating from university and starting a teaching job. Then she fulfilled her own dream by quitting teaching and earning a living as a writer.

Mary Quant was developing her highly successful fashion business, beginning to export designs to the USA and selling lots of mini skirts.

Kath Fincham was campaigning for trade union rights for women. In 1969 she led a march for bus conductresses to win the right to become drivers.

Barbara Castle was a cabinet minister in the Labour government from 1965. Her responsibilities at different times covered transport, trade unions and employment.

Daphne Steele was working as matron at a hospital in West Yorkshire, having arrived from Guyana in 1951. She was Britain's first black matron.

Dorothy Hodgkin was becoming one of the world's most respected chemists, winning the Nobel Prize in 1964.

Yet how typical were the women on this page? Were most women, by contrast, happy to stay at home in the traditional roles of wife and mother? The two statistical summaries on page 77 provide an overall picture.

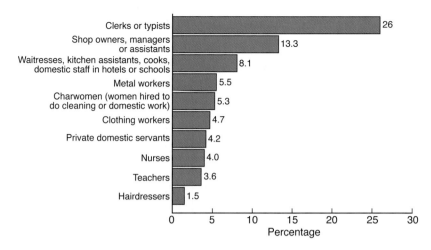

◁ **The most common jobs for women in 1966 as a percentage of all working women.**

A professor of chemistry interviewed about the education of girls commented in 1964 that, 'In my experience most girls simply don't have the right sort of brains for chemistry.'

Women in the labour force in Great Britain 1951–81				
	1951	1961	1971	1981
Women in labour force (% of total labour force)	31	33	37	40
Women in labour force (% of women aged 20–64)	36	42	52	61
Women employed part time (% of women aged 20–64)	12	26	35	42
Married women in labour force (% of all married women aged 15–59)	26	35	49	62

These statistics indicate a steady increase in the proportion of women going out to work between 1951 and 1981. The biggest rise was for married women, with many of them taking up part-time jobs. The 1960s decade shows significant increases in women working but this is clearly part of a trend started in the 1950s and which continued in the 1970s. The largest increases in female employment were in the clerical and retail sphere. Businesses had 'typing pools', employing large numbers of mostly young women using the new electronic typewriters to process their documents. Many married women worked part time in the newly created supermarkets or had jobs as receptionists, telephonists or cleaners. The 1960s expansion of university education opened up more professions for women but this did not have an immediate impact. Only a minority of dentists, doctors, architects or accountants were female and this remained true for decades to come.

Clearly, women's lives changed after the war but opportunities differed according to class and race. Asian and Afro-Caribbean families were more reliant on women's earnings although they often worked in low-paid jobs. Some poorly educated working-class girls had limited job opportunities compared to young women in middle-class families with university and professional careers on the horizon. On the whole, women became healthier, wealthier and better educated. They worked in the home and outside and, by the mid-1970s, were not condemned for doing so. **Companionate marriage** was the ideal for most couples. By this time women had rights to equal pay, to employment choices, to protected income on divorce and to maternity leave.

Women were not awarded degrees from Cambridge University on equal terms with men until 1948. In 2002, for the first time, more women than men gained places for a degree course at Cambridge.

companionate marriage
A view of marriage as a partnership of equals, with husband and wife both able to pursue careers and share chores and childcare

77

Changes in employment law: two more shaky moments

Equal Pay Act 1970

What it said

Women should be paid the same as men in equivalent work. Employers were given five years to implement it.

What it did

Five years after the Act was implemented the average hourly pay of all women workers was 59 per cent of men's – the same as it was in the 1960s. The British workforce was highly sex segregated – around 80 per cent of men and women worked in jobs that were dominated by one gender and in these employment areas the new rules had little impact. Employers found ways round implementing them by redefining jobs to make comparisons more difficult. The Act only worked effectively in areas of employment where men and women worked side by side in similar roles, such as factory production.

In 1983 the law was toughened up so that work of 'equal value' had to receive equal pay. This Act had more impact – by the mid-80s women were getting 74 per cent of the pay of men.

Sex Discrimination Act 1975

What it said

It was unlawful for an employer to discriminate against a worker on grounds of sex or marital status.

What it did

In theory, it opened up many employment opportunities previously closed to women such as engineering, printing and transport. In practice it was difficult and expensive for women to pursue their cases in the courts. In 1976 only five out of twenty sex discrimination cases were successful.

From my own experience I feel there is much to be said for being away from the family for part of the day.

(Quotation from 27-year-old housewife, Margaret Thatcher, defending working wives in 1954. She became Britain's first female prime minister in 1979)

Did this mean that women were now equal to men? It seems this took much longer, if it ever happened at all. While laws on employment and rights changed, traditional behaviour did not. Female teachers won equal pay with men in 1961 yet their average pay deteriorated in the following ten years. Were they passed over for promotion or did they choose lower hours and lower status in order to put family first? Very few men helped in the home; it was women who cleaned the toilets and met the children from school. A 1980s survey showed that most men and women believed that married women should prioritise the demands of the home before paid work. There were more female workers, graduates, employers and campaigners in the 1960s and 1970s. But in British homes, there needed to be more male nappy changers, cooks and cleaners for gender roles to be seriously shaken up. It was not until the twenty-first century that surveys suggest this was beginning to happen.

Now reflect on the main trends in female employment and assess how far women's work changed and when these changes occurred.

1 Make notes in answer to the following questions and then use them to make your judgement on the 'shockometer'.

   a What were the key changes in women's work between 1950 and 1980?

   b How far did these changes occur in the 1960s rather than before or after?

   c What was the nature and extent of these changes? Note differences between age groups, ethnicity and class.

2 Use your notes on a–c to decide where you judge the topic 'Female employment' should go on the 'shockometer'.

Did feminism make an impact?

◁ Protestors at the Miss World contest in 1970.

Active feminism: the Women's Liberation Movement

The 25 million viewers who switched on the Miss World contest in 1970 were in for a surprise. Televised live, the contestants paraded in their national costumes and evening dress. In their swimsuits they obediently followed the instruction to face the wall so that their rear views could be assessed. The American celebrity, Bob Hope, took the stage and made some jokes. And then the feminists made their move. The Albert Hall in London was disrupted with whistles and rattles; flour and tomatoes soon littered the stage. Banners were unfurled. 'We're not beautiful, we're not ugly, we're angry,' the protesters announced. Women's Liberation had arrived in British family living rooms.

This incident raises one of the key issues for the women's movement of the time. For the so-called 'second wave' **feminists** of the 1960s and 1970s, Miss World was a showpiece for the exploitation of women by the profitable and male-dominated entertainment business, Mecca. A few months earlier women had gathered in Oxford at the first National Women's Liberation Conference to agree their four key goals (see the table on page 82). The year 1970 proved pivotal in the development of women's rights.

In the 1960s women had supported campaigns for reform in the laws on divorce and abortion and welcomed greater opportunities in education. In 1963 Betty Friedan's book, *The Feminine Mystique*, created a furore in the United States by claiming that intelligent women were unhappily trapped in their lives as wives and mothers. Yet this book had limited impact on most British women in the 1960s, with many young women choosing to marry and have children in their early twenties, apparently welcoming conventional domesticity.

In Britain, there can be little doubt that it was in the 1970s that the Women's Liberation Movement hit the headlines and made a real impact. Feminists led campaigns for equal pay and job opportunities, attacked sex shops and pornography and brought to light the suffering of women through domestic violence and rape.

But were most British women angry? At its peak, the Women's Liberation Movement probably only attracted around 10,000 activists. It became increasingly divided during the 1970s, with Marxist, lesbian and other splinter groups developing different views on issues such as the family, marriage and work.

feminists
First-wave feminists were those who campaigned for changes in the law such as equal pay, whereas second-wave feminists turned their attention to other issues such as the family and sexuality

Cultural feminism: the impact of feminist writing

While some feminists promoted the rights of women through marches and campaigns, others tried to change attitudes by writing. One key publication was Germaine Greer's *The Female Eunuch*.

Germaine Greer and *The Female Eunuch*

Written in a forthright style, Greer's breakthrough work called on women to reject the traditional passive roles assigned to them in conventional family life and to fight for sexual and economic independence. Greer was an Australian academic who loved to shock: she admitted to wearing no underwear and carrying around a velvet bag full of coloured condoms.

Extract

> Maybe I don't have a pretty smile, good teeth, nice tits, long legs, a cheeky arse, a sexy voice. Maybe I don't know how to handle men and increase my market value, so that the rewards due to the feminine will accrue to me. Then again, maybe I'm sick of the masquerade. I'm sick of pretending eternal youth. I'm sick of belying my own intelligence, my own will, my own sex. I'm sick of peering at the world through false eyelashes, so everything I see is mixed with a shadow of bought hairs; I'm sick of weighting my head with a dead mane, unable to move my neck freely, terrified of rain, of wind, of dancing too vigorously in case I sweat into my lacquered curls. I'm sick of the Powder Room. I'm sick of pretending that some fatuous male's self-important pronouncements are the objects of my undivided attention, I'm sick of going to films and plays when someone else wants to, and sick of having no opinions of my own about either. I'm sick of being a transvestite. I refuse to be a female impersonator. I am a woman, not a castrate.

Impact

This book was an instant sensation after its publication in 1970, selling a million copies worldwide and never going out of print. The book influenced many women to re-think their lives, especially in middle-class households.

Below is one woman's reaction:

> I read it in 1973, when I was thirteen and it shaped my whole life. I can remember very clearly the light bulb moment, while reading it, when I realised that if I didn't make my own money, I would always have to ask my husband for the cash if I wanted to buy a new dress. And that I might have to be nice to him and agree with things he said, that I didn't believe in, and have sex with him even if I didn't feel like it, and make what he wanted for dinner even if I didn't want it, to get that money. Ping!
>
> (Maggie Alderson)

In order to put this book in context, it is worth considering what most British women were reading in the 1960s and 1970s. Romantic fiction was the most popular choice and these were boom years for the publisher Mills and Boon. These stories always focused on finding a suitable man, with the heroine playing a submissive role. One of their leading writers wrote a description of her typical hero in 1970:

> … they're lean and hard muscled and mocking and sardonic and tough and tigerish and single, of course. Oh and they've got to be rich and then I make it that they're only cynical and smooth on the surface. But underneath they're well, you know, sort of lost and lonely. In need of love but, when roused, capable of breathtaking passion and potency. Most of my heroes, well all of them really, are like that. They frighten but fascinate. They must be the sort of men who are capable of rape: men it's dangerous to be alone in the room with.
>
> (Violet Winspear)

△ A traditional Mills and Boon book cover from the 1970s.

Most of the best-selling women's magazines also seemed blithely unaware of feminist thinking. In 1969 more than 30 per cent of women were reading either *Woman* or *Woman's Own* on a weekly basis. Around 60 per cent of non-beauty articles in the three leading women's magazines in the 1960s were on the themes of 'Getting and Keeping your Man'. A survey of *Honey* readers in 1978 showed that what they truly wanted was 'a husband, a home (preferably detached and in the country), and two children'. It was enough, the editor remarked, to make Ms Greer pack her bags and go home to Australia.

Study of female reading habits raises as many questions as it answers. Readers of Greer tended to be better off and better educated; already half persuaded by feminism. Thousands of women curled up on their sofas to escape into the world of Mills and Boon or enjoy a light-hearted article in *Woman*. Many of them were middle aged and on middle or low incomes. But readers have minds of their own. Few women walked out on their families to follow a feminist vision of equality. Fewer still believed that their lives would be transformed by romance with an exotic stranger. Both Greer's call to action and the Mills and Boon fantasy served as strong contrasts to the everyday reality of most women's lives.

Perhaps the real achievement of the feminists in this era was to raise awareness of women's issues. Sensitive social issues such as rape were publicly discussed. Secretaries gained the confidence to speak out against their boss's sexual harassment. Women began to challenge the sexism of advertising. Few women, even by the end of the 1970s, were actively involved in the feminist movement. Bra burning never really took off. Yet feminism gave women a more confident and louder voice in British society.

Alex's voice rubbed against her like warm velvet. Deena had to consciously hold in a shiver, while she attempted a cool, sophisticated expression.

(from *A Fool For Love*, a Mills and Boon title)

Fay Weldon, the novelist, talking about courtship in the 1950s: 'We were meant to be virgins but seldom were. Then, as now, women were searching for Mr Right, a man who was their superior in status, wealth and education.'

A divisive issue of the 1970s: the Wages for Housework Campaign
If the government paid housewives a salary, feminists argued, they could become truly independent and receive the respect their work merited. Other women's campaigners argued that this would confirm the view that domestic chores were women's work and allow men off the hook! Partly due to these disagreements, the campaign never really took off.

Key developments

1963	Betty Friedan's *The Feminine Mystique* was published in the USA.
1970	The Women's Liberation Movement met for the first time at Ruskin College, Oxford. They passed unanimous resolutions on four key demands: equal pay; equal education and opportunity; 24-hour nurseries; free contraception and abortion on demand.
	Germaine Greer's *The Female Eunuch* was published.
	Disruption to the Miss World contest.
1971	The National Women's Liberation Movement organised their first march in London.
	Erin Pizzey set up the first refuge for female victims of domestic violence in Chiswick in London. From around this time feminists drew attention to the issue of male violence towards women, especially rape and wife battering.
1972	The first edition of *Spare Rib*, the feminist magazine, was published.
1975	There were more than 1500 women's liberation groups meeting around the country.
1979	The Southall Black Sisters was founded to fight domestic violence and unfair legal treatment for black women.

Use these pages to evaluate the impact of feminism on British society

1 Consider the following questions and then use them to make your judgement on the 'shockometer'.

   a What were the main developments in the feminist movement in the 1960s?

   b In what ways did (i) active and (ii) cultural feminism make progress in the 1970s?

   c What were the limitations in the progress of feminism to 1980?

2 Use your notes on a–c to decide where you judge the topic 'Impact of feminism' should go on the 'shockometer'.

When were attitudes to homosexuals shaken up?

In March 1954, at the Winchester Assizes, three men were found guilty and sentenced to prison. The defendants were a lord, his cousin and the *Daily Mail's* diplomatic correspondent. The sensational trial had attracted a huge crowd of press and public. The police, worried about the men's safety, kept them in their cells for two hours, hoping people would disperse. They didn't. But when the men finally emerged from the court house on their way to prison, they were greeted with claps and cheers.

Until 1967 any act of homosexuality was illegal in the UK. Lord Montagu of Beaulieu and his two friends had just been convicted of gross indecency yet the public reaction suggested that the law was out of tune with public opinion. Yet some have argued that homosexuality was legalised before the general public approved:

> ... the Sexual Offences Act ... gave a lead to public opinion that was still stuck in the dark days of the 1950s, kick-starting a transformation in attitudes that would become a revolution.
>
> (*The Guardian*, 28 July 2007)

Government policy, gay activism and shifts in public opinion have all played a part in the changes listed below. Although the most important legal change came in 1967, changes in people's attitudes altered much more slowly.

A shake up in the law?

- The government-sponsored Wolfenden Report (1957) recommended that homosexual acts in private between consenting adults should no longer be an offence. The government chose not to act.
- The Sexual Offences Act was passed in 1967, allowing homosexual acts in private. It did not cover Scotland and Northern Ireland, set an age of consent of 21 (compared to sixteen for heterosexuals) and homosexuality was still illegal in the armed forces.
- A police clampdown followed the Act with a doubling of incidents of public indecency between males and a trebling of prosecutions in the years 1967–76.
- Homosexuality was only legalised in Scotland in 1980, Northern Ireland in 1982, and in 1992 on the Isle of Man.
- By 2005, homosexuals were legally protected from discrimination, could enter civil partnerships and had the same age of consent as heterosexuals.

A shake up in public attitudes?

- 5000 copies of the report were sold immediately. It was supported by the Archbishop of Canterbury, seven national newspapers and the British Medical Association.
- Leading Christians condemned permissive attitudes to homosexuality at the National Festival of Light in 1971, an event organised to improve public morality.

- The outbreak of AIDs in the early 1980s still led to hostile press coverage and increased homophobia.

- In 1987 Margaret Thatcher and other Conservatives condemned liberal views of homosexuality which they believed was being promoted in schools.

- In 1969 research suggested only 12 per cent of the public had a tolerant view of homosexuality. Later social attitude surveys show that 62 per cent thought homosexuality should be tolerated in society in 1983, rising to more than 70 per cent by 2007. A study of homosexuals in 2006, however, showed that 40 per cent had been victims of abuse.

A shake up in homosexual behaviour?

- In 1958 a group of mainly middle-class men set up the Homosexual Law Reform Society to campaign for a change in the law.

- The Gay Liberation Front was set up in 1971 to actively campaign for gay rights. The first Gay Pride rally involving 1000 people took place in London in the following year.

- From the 1980s public figures, such as the gay MP Chris Smith, began to talk more openly about their sexuality.

- By 2005 there was an open and active 'gay scene' in most UK cities.

Shaking up people's lives: the life stories of two gay actors

Sir John Gielgud (1904–2000)

importuning
Requesting homosexual or immoral acts

Gielgud was a distinguished Shakespearean actor, who was knighted in 1953. Shortly after this he was arrested in a public lavatory in Chelsea on a charge of **importuning**. He pleaded guilty, was fined £10 and hoped, by using the name 'Arthur' and wearing horn-rimmed glasses, he had escaped press attention. But he was not so lucky. A journalist recognised his distinctive deep voice in court and the story hit the headlines.

△ Sir John Gielgud playing Hamlet.

Gielgud briefly contemplated suicide, thought his career ruined and that he would have to immediately quit acting. His fellow actors encouraged him to carry on and his mother forgave him as long as the incident was 'never mentioned again'. The public reaction was divided: he received several abusive letters and a cold reception on stage in Edinburgh but in London he was given a standing ovation.

Gielgud had several long-term relationships with men during his successful career as actor and director. He secretly gave money to the gay rights group Stonewall but refused ever to talk publicly about his sexuality. Finally, in 1988, he allowed the comment in theatre programme notes that he had been living happily with his partner Martin Hensler for many years. Gielgud died in 2000. The day after his death theatre lights in London's West End were dimmed in his memory.

John Inman (1935–2007)

Inman was an actor who became well known for his roles in comedy and pantomime in the 1970s and 1980s. He was best known for his role as Mr Humphries in the popular sitcom *Are You Being Served?*, which was set in an old-fashioned department store. His character was deliberately **camp**, in contrast to Gielgud's more circumspect approach, although Mr Humphries's sexuality was never directly mentioned. Although the BBC had been worried about the inclusion of such an overtly 'camp' character, Mr Humphries proved a great success. He was voted the funniest man on television in 1976 and also won the BBC Television Personality of the Year award.

△ John Inman (left) as Mr Humphries in the sitcom *Are You Being Served?*

camp
Acting or behaving in an openly effeminate way

Some gay activists found the stereotypical portrayal of Mr Humphries offensive and picketed one of his shows in protest. Inman justified his role, insisting that it was not over the top and that Humphries was just 'a mother's boy'.

Inman entered into a civil partnership with his long-term partner Ron Lynch in 2005 and under the new laws was able to leave him a substantial legacy on his death in 2007.

You now need to sum up when and how far attitudes to homosexuality have changed.

1 Consider the following questions and then use them to make your judgement on the 'shockometer'.

  a What evidence is there that attitudes to homosexuality had begun to change before the 1960s?

  b How significant were the changes in the 1960s decade? Consider the law, public attitudes and the actions of homosexuals themselves.

  c What evidence is there that the main changes have happened since the 1960s? Use the same headings of law, public attitudes and the actions of the gay community.

2 Use your notes on a–c to decide where you judge the topic 'Attitudes to homosexuality' should go on the 'shockometer'.

Review: Was sex shaken up in the 1960s?

The 1960s were *the* pivotal decade. Until then there were no certain methods of contraception under the control of women. The discovery and subsequent availability of oral contraception, intra-uterine devices and, at the end of the decade, long-term injectables and implants, were fundamental to subsequent changes in social attitudes. It became possible to separate reproduction and sexual intercourse. For the first time, women were no longer under the dominion of men. All previous legislative attempts to bring equality had failed individual women as long as the possibility of pregnancy was beyond their control. The Abortion Act (1967) logically closed the last loophole to sexual equality with men.

These facts took most of the decade to percolate through into changed social attitudes. In 1960 bearing a child outside marriage was social suicide. Sex was only acceptable within marriage. By 1970 not only was it accepted as normal within a long-term relationship between men and women but it was no longer illegal for those of the same sex.

The 1970s cemented these attitudes not only with legislation (free family planning within the NHS from 1974), changes in the professional attitudes of the medical profession and young people being free to seek advice without parental consent but also with single parenthood no longer being shameful (the closure of 'Mother and Baby Homes'). The foundations of all these changes were laid in the scientific advances of the 1960s.

△ The author's mother, Dr Libby Wilson, in 2012.

This is my mother's verdict on the importance of the 1960s. As a retired family planning doctor, and the mother of six children, she might be regarded as an expert witness. But do other experts agree with her view?

That there were immense changes in British sexual attitudes and behaviour in the late twentieth century is indisputable. There is compelling evidence of radical shifts in patterns of marriage, illegitimacy and female employment. Public opinion and British law softened on homosexuality, divorce and abortion. The 1960s were a pivotal decade for changes in the law yet it was often not until later decades that social acceptance followed suit. There is still no general agreement, however, about the nature, pace and extent of change. Why?

When evaluating complex issues such as this, students seek uncomplicated and clear historical judgements. It is much simpler to plan an essay when one historian strongly supports one viewpoint and another strongly disagrees. But historians are not like tennis players, hitting shots to catch their opponent out. It is rare for them to adopt completely opposing views. More often they work collaboratively, passing the 'historical ball' about, adding different perspectives and materials to create a more complete picture of the past. Moreover, criticising a historian because their research only covers one angle or view suggests a flawed understanding of how historians work. Few set out to provide history students with a comprehensive account of an era or topic; most have the more modest aim of throwing light on one particular area or aspect of the past. It is then unsurprising that general judgements are rarely agreed.

Read the points below to understand why historians might emerge with different views.

1   **The particular specialism or perspective of the historian.** Usually academic historians choose one area of history to study in depth, following their own skills and interests. In the field of sexual history, for instance, there may be historians whose focus is mainly medical, studying national health surveys and clinical records, while another may be looking at the cultural angle, considering how sexual issues were addressed in the arts and media.

    Example: Matt Houlbrook's book *Queer London: Perils and Pleasures in the Sexual Metropolis 1918–1957* (2006) tells the story of the lives of homosexuals in London, uncovering new evidence about the gay community in the capital, and revealing new evidence in a completely fresh approach to sexual history.

2   **The evidence base and the main sources of information used.** Some historians make great use of statistical evidence, such as national data, while others rely more on personal evidence such as diaries and letters.

    Example: For her study of teenage sexuality, *Feminism and Youth Culture* (1991), Angela Robbie researched teenage magazines in the 1960s and 1970s to understand adolescent views and ideas. This gave her a rich well of information about teenage girls' sexual attitudes at that time.

3   **The methodology, how the historian conducted his or her research.** While all professional historians accept the same general code of conduct, such as using evidence honestly and including correct references, there are great differences in how they might conduct their research. In the field of sexual history, some historians have relied mainly on general surveys using a full range of national and local records while others may choose to rely mostly on one kind of source such as family planning records.

    Example: Kate Fisher, in her book *Birth Control, Sex, and Marriage in Britain 1918–1960* (2006), was the first British historian to use oral history as the main research basis for a book on sexual history. She argues persuasively that these recorded interviews provided evidence that challenged written records and gave new insights into the intimate lives of couples.

4   **The values and beliefs of the historian.** Historians are individuals with their own political, moral and religious outlook. These beliefs sometimes influence their writing directly and obviously and sometimes in more subtle ways. Committed feminists, for instance, strongly promoted the study of women's history from the 1970s onwards, with the desire to address the gender imbalance of historical writing in the past.

    Example: Sheila Rowbotham is a pioneer of the Women's Liberation Movement and a committed Marxist. Her book *Century of Women: The History of Women in Britain and the United States in the Twentieth Century* (2000) is written from this perspective, tracing the struggle of working-class women in particular to fight injustice and oppression.

Good history students will read the writings of many different historians before reaching their conclusions. The process of reaching these judgements is more like selecting a range of items from a buffet than choosing one dish from a menu. All the research above contributes to a picture of sexual and social change while none on its own gives you a concrete or comprehensive view of the key question you are exploring. Once again, this highlights the complexity of modern social history and the need to reach several qualified judgements rather than attempt an overall generalisation.

Returning to the issue of whether the 1960s was the key decade of social change, these points are illustrated by the studies of the two historians below. They concern different aspects of social and sexual changes in this period and offer contrasting views of the nature and extent of change.

Extract 1

The introduction of reliable contraception is one among many changes that increased the control of fear, and allowed a greater experience of pleasure and increased emotional aspirations. There have been substantial improvements, amounting to a transformation, in the lives of English women over the past two centuries. The generation of women who came of age in the 1950s and the early 1960s lived through a period in which this process came to a head and female sexual **mores** were transformed.

(from *The Long Sexual Revolution: English Women, Sex and Contraception in England 1800–1975* (2004), a study of the links between sex, fertility and women's lives over nearly 200 years)

mores
Customs or characteristics

The author

Hera Cook is an academic at the University of Birmingham who specialises in the history of women, children and sexuality. In her research she relied heavily on fertility statistics, sex manuals and surveys. She studied in depth the impact of contraception on relationships, placing great weight on the ability of women to control their own fertility for the first time with the advent of the contraceptive pill.

Comment

Cook is particularly focusing on the impact of the pill, putting this in the context of a long overview of women and birth control over time. Her study of national data over time leads her to conclude that there was a major transformation in women's lives in the post-war decades.

Extract 2

Studies of the way sex roles have changed in recent years show that they have undergone no radical reversal. Most changes (such as the increasing employment of women) have been superficial, failing to affect the traditional balance of relationships between the sexes and the traditional definitions of gender roles.

(from *Sex, Gender and Society* (1972) in which the author used evidence from biology and anthropology to examine issues of sex and gender in a range of different societies and times)

The author

Ann Oakley is a sociologist who specialises in issues of sex and gender. She was one of the most outspoken feminist writers and researchers in the 1960s and 1970s. Oakley was the first researcher to investigate housework as a serious academic study. She challenged the underlying assumptions of many writers that physical gender differences necessarily led to set roles and behaviour for men and women.

Comment

Oakley considers the role of women in a much broader context, using her studies of anatomy and anthropology. Writing in 1972 she has a strong feminist view of changes that were happening in the years just before she wrote the book. From this perspective, it is not surprising that she concludes that progress towards sexual equality has been insignificant.

It would make no sense to state that one of these views is right and the other wrong nor to comment that one is 'reliable' and the other not. One writer is focused much more on sexual behaviour while the other is considering gender roles. The value of their writing would depend on the question you are asking. For this chapter's main question, 'Were the "swinging sixties" the time of most change?', neither extract gives a straightforward answer although both help you to answer it. Hera Cook adds weight to the view that the pill transformed the private sexual lives of many women. Ann Oakley confirms the frustrations of feminists that true sexual equality was still a faraway goal in 1972. That neither interpretation gives you a simple verdict is just a reflection of the complexity of history. From these two studies you might reasonably conclude that:

1   Contraception had a major impact on the sexual and emotional lives of women from the early 1960s onwards.

2   Women's opportunities, especially in the workplace, did not greatly change until after the 1960s.

This illustrates how historians can help you to make a series of judgements that complement each other to build a strong conclusion.

It is now time to review the chapter's main question: Were the 'swinging sixties' the time of most change? Go through the following before reaching your final judgements:

1 Review all the points on your shockometer to sum up:

   a which changes occurred in the 1960s

   b which were part of a preceding trend

   c which developed later.

2 Review and consider the comments on interpretations given in this chapter.

3 Instead of trying to come up with one general judgement, write down three or four conclusions about how far the 1960s were the time of most change. Consider the nature and extent of change, such as which aspects changed the most and the least and which women were most affected by them.

A closer look at statistics and surveys

Statistics are often judged to be the most reliable form of historical evidence. They are, apparently, factual and objective, mostly coming from trustworthy sources such as governments or research surveys. Of course, it is possible to manipulate and edit figures just like text, but this is usually thought to be a problem only when the numbers are the product of pressure groups or dictatorships.

But is it all as simple as that? The study below shows the dangers of using statistics uncritically.

A study

These are the responses of a mass observation street survey of 1949 asking whether people were in favour of birth control.

Approve	63%
Disapprove	15%
Other (mixed feelings, refused to reply, don't know or irrelevant)	22%

So we can confidently conclude that, even by 1949, a comfortable majority of British people supported the option of birth control. Or can we?

Putting aside the possible lack of balanced representation that might be expected from a random street survey, an earlier question in the same survey raises doubts about the validity of the responses. When asked what birth control meant, only 71 per cent of the answers were correct. Some thought it meant giving birth, others that it was abortion. More than 95 per cent of those who did not know what it meant had left school before the age of fourteen. This raises questions about whether the responses above provided an accurate reflection of working-class views. Those who answered confidently were more likely to be middle class, a group that was generally more liberal in social attitudes anyway. Does this make the evidence invalid? No, the responses of more than 2000 people selected at random provide invaluable information for historians. It's just a reminder that all evidence, including statistics, needs to be used with care and caution.

When using statistical evidence, there is a range of factors worth considering when weighing up the evidence provided:

- Selection of sample (i.e. those completing the survey): voluntary or compulsory, self selection or random selection.
- The range and representation of the sample, i.e. class, region, age, ethnicity, gender, religion.
- The methods used by the researcher, e.g. oral or written records, anonymous or identified responses, the phrasing of the questions posed.
- The purpose of the survey, e.g. commercial or academic.

The following examples highlight some of the strengths and limitations of statistical evidence. This simply confirms that numerical data must be treated cautiously and critically like all historical evidence. And like all historical material, its value depends largely on the question the historian is asking.

Examples

National government data

1   Social Attitudes surveys: From 1983 the government commissioned an annual Social Attitudes survey which covers attitudes and beliefs on a range of issues from a random sample of the population.

2   The government collects large amounts of data through registration of births, marriages and deaths, the electoral roll (which records information about all people who are entitled to vote) and the census. The census is a compulsory survey completed every ten years (the years ending '1') by every household, leading to more than 90 per cent of people providing information about their jobs, families and living standards. Until 2001, it asked no questions about opinions, lifestyle choices or beliefs. Government data is collected by the Office of Population Censuses and Surveys (OPCS) which publishes regular reports such as Social Trends.

Comment

Government data can be especially useful as the state can make everyone provide information for the purpose of providing an accurate national overview. For objective information about trends across the country, these statistics are hard to beat but the nature of the survey questions mean they have limited use for understanding changes in intimate and private matters.

Academic research survey

Michael Schofield, a Cambridge-educated psychologist, conducted his academic research project, Sexual Behaviour of Young People, in two phases: a study of teenagers in 1965 and a follow-up study of the same cohort published in 1973. Supported by government and academic bodies, the survey was based on more than 1800 interviews with a representative sample of teenagers from different areas of the country. Only around 15 per cent of the randomly chosen sample refused to answer the questions which covered a range of intimate and personal matters. He claimed his report was the 'most thorough and valid sexual research ever carried out in this country'.

Comment

The rigorous research methods used for this project, in particular the random nature of the sample and very high levels of compliance, mean that the findings are widely accepted. For historians studying teenage sexual behaviour between 1965 and 1973 Schofield's data is undoubtedly an invaluable source. Yet Schofield's work does not provide a comprehensive picture of teenage sexual habits. He has been criticised for neglecting homosexual relations and sexual activity that was not full intercourse. So while the methods make this evidence particularly valuable, the questions asked limit the scope of the evidence provided.

Magazine surveys

From the 1970s reader surveys became a common part of best-selling magazines such as Woman's Own. Their purpose was mainly to provide an interesting follow-up feature for readers. Large numbers of women would respond, for instance in 1975, 10,000 women sent their answers to 'Your Marriage – the Truth at Last' in Woman's Own. The process was completely anonymous and the questions often personal, explicit and probing, e.g. would you marry a different man if you could? Experts were often used to summarise and analyse the results. Magazine circulation varied greatly according to class and age. Woman and Woman's Own achieved circulations of more than 2 million weekly in the 1960s and 1970s, their readers mainly being women on average incomes in the 25–40 age bracket.

Comment

The anonymous nature of these surveys and the style of questions asked provided information about the private relationships of married couples that is hard to match from other sources. These surveys provide useful insight into the attitudes and behaviour of lower- and middle-class women in their twenties and thirties. It should be remembered, however, that the survey respondents were willing volunteers, not a random sample, and therefore may not be typical, even of women's magazine readers. The reliance on willing volunteers and the limited range of the magazine circulation means that this evidence needs to be treated with some caution.

Has the British media been a unifying force?

In the summer of 1982 Britain was at war. Argentina had attacked the Falkland Islands and Prime Minister Margaret Thatcher had sent a naval task force to reclaim them. Thatcher's determined response to the crisis was widely praised. The troops were waved off from the docks in a mass of patriotic flags. In the offices of Britain's best-selling newspaper, *The Sun*, the news editor wore a naval cap and placed a picture of Winston Churchill on the wall. Single-word patriotic headlines dominated their news coverage. The sinking of the Argentinian cruiser, the *General Belgrano*, on 2 May, was the first major encounter between the two enemies, and one of the most dramatic actions of the war, with the loss of 368 Argentinian lives. *The Sun*'s front page was dominated by large, bold letters spelling out 'Gotcha'.

The Sun represented the most extreme reporting of the Falklands War but other media, including the BBC, also adopted a patriotic tone. The Ministry of Defence strictly controlled access to information but they had little to worry about. Max Hastings, who won an award for his reporting from the Falklands, stated that the journalist's role was 'simply to report as sympathetically as possible what the British forces are doing here today'. He justified this statement by quoting his father who had been a correspondent in the Second World War: 'When one's nation is at war, reporting becomes an extension of the war effort.' Margaret Thatcher and her Tory government became more popular than ever before.

From this you might conclude that the wartime media played an important part in unifying the nation. But it is not as simple as that. The popular *Daily Mirror* and the broadsheet newspaper *The Guardian* adopted a much more critical stance. And modern research suggests that *The Sun*'s **jingoism** probably lost them sales. On their ships to the Falklands some soldiers burnt copies of the paper to show their disgust at its coverage. Margaret Thatcher was plainly rattled in a television debate when a housewife challenged the legality of the *Belgrano* sinking. So, far from creating an uncritical consensus behind the war, it appears the media exposed the divisions and criticisms of the public as well.

Wars give the media a crucial role. Yet the complexity of the media's role in the Falklands War extends to the relationship between media and society generally. The sharing of national events on television, such as royal weddings, national football matches, and even the plots of popular soaps, can contribute to a common language and culture. But up until the 1980s, at least, the British media was dominated by white men, many educated at public school. There were few black faces presenting the news, Irish accents on the radio or women writing sports reports for the papers. Intense competition in the media usually meant pleasing the masses at the expense of the minorities. The British media has, at different times, been accused of being racist, sexist and immoral. Has the media helped to shape modern 'Britishness'? Or has it just reflected a narrow and nostalgic view of the Britain of the past?

jingoism
Aggressive and extreme nationalism

In his short-lived rule of the Falklands, the Argentinian governor tried to win over the inhabitants with a promise of a colour television in every household in time for the football World Cup. Clearly he was in no doubt about the importance of the media.

This book raises many tricky questions about social history but these are probably the hardest of all to answer. It is not so difficult to survey how the media has portrayed British society and how press reporting and television programmes have changed in the way they present social issues. It is possible to reach some valid conclusions from social attitudes surveys, about how British views on sex, race and morality have developed over time. But to relate one to the other is hugely problematic. If the early episodes of the police series *The Bill* portrayed police officers as white and criminals as black, it is likely that this confirmed negative views of the black community. But it is almost impossible to prove. It seems plausible that the publication of bare-breasted girls on page 3 of *The Sun* affected attitudes to women. But in what way and how much? The royal wedding of spring 2011 was watched by a huge proportion of Britons, of all races and backgrounds. But how long did this mood of patriotic unity last? The evidence on these issues is patchy and inconclusive. Modern social historians, as this book has suggested, are cautious about reaching firm, overarching judgements. In this chapter in particular, suggestions and theories will often be more appropriate than rigid conclusions.

■ **Enquiry Focus:** Has the British media been a unifying force?

As you work your way through this chapter consider how far the media has been a force for unity or disunity in Britain under the following headings:

- **Nationality** Use this heading to judge how far the media has helped the British to share a sense of belonging to one country. You might consider, on the one hand, the way the media has enabled Britons to share national occasions such as royal weddings. On the other hand, the media may have served to re-affirm a narrow or exclusive view of the nation, for instance by providing TV coverage of the Boat Race but not the Notting Hill Carnival.

- **Class** You will need to consider the ways different social groups are portrayed in the media and whether this has broken down or re-enforced class barriers. Control of the media for most of the past 60 years has been largely in the hands of middle-class graduates and wealthy businessmen. How far this has affected stereotypical views of social classes will be a key issue in this chapter.

- **Race** The media has had a big influence over British race relations. There are important differences here between the 'print media' (newspapers) and radio, film and television. In this chapter, you will need to judge how different parts of the media have portrayed ethnic minorities and how this has affected attitudes to racial groups and immigration.

- **Values** There were major changes in ideas about morality in this time and most believe that the media played a key role in this. The debate about the 'permissive society' and how far attitudes to sex, morals and language were changed by the media is an important part of this chapter.

Has the media been a force for unity or disunity in Britain?

Unity	Disunity
Press support for the Falklands War, especially from *The Sun*, fostered a patriotic mood and support for Thatcher's government.	Criticism of the Falklands War increased after Thatcher appeared to falter when challenged on television by a member of the public.

Sketch the diagram on the left on a large piece of paper. Then add precise notes from each topic in this chapter, justifying their place on the continuum line. Use a highlighter to colour code the different categories listed above. Two points from the introductory section have been included as examples to help you get started.

Major changes in access to and consumption of the media 1945–2005

It is obvious from the information on this spread that the rate of change in the media has speeded up dramatically in the last 50 years. There were experiments with colour television broadcasting in 1954 but it was not until 1967 that colour televisions were available for British viewers. Changes in new technologies have developed at a much faster rate, for example the meteoric rise in the use of computers and the internet. One notable aspect of these changes is the inter-connectivity of the media and new technology. Newspaper articles are read online, television programmes are viewed on computer screens and radio programmes downloaded onto iPods.

Television

1947 9 per cent of UK households had a TV

1953 25 per cent had a TV

1972 93 per cent had a TV

2002 99 per cent had a TV

1955 ITV started broadcasting, ending BBC monopoly

1982 Channel 4 began

1990 the British Broadcasting Act introduced satellite and cable television

2002 44 per cent of households had satellite, cable or digital television

1967 colour broadcasting started

1980s portable televisions introduced and VCRs (video recorders) became common

Cinema

1946 peak attendance with more than 1.6 billion annual admissions to the cinema

1959 580 million attendance

1984 a low point of 55 million

late 1980s and 1990s development of multiplex cinemas

1991 attendance recovered to 100 million

2005 attendance reached 164 million

Radio

Emerged from war as main home news and entertainment service

1946 BBC Radio broadcast three stations, 10.5 million radio licences issued

1960s commercial Radio Luxembourg and pirate Radio Caroline were popular rival radio stations to BBC

1967 launch of Radio 1

1970s development of local commercial radio

1990s more deregulation

1992 launch of Classic FM

1971 radio licences abolished

Technological developments:

1960s portable transistors

1970s car radios

1990s digital radio

Newspapers

Newspaper circulation:

1950s and 1960s the *Daily Mirror* achieved daily sales of 5 million

1969 *The Sun* relaunched, establishing a daily circulation of 4 million by 1978

Decline in provincial press:

1980s advent of free local papers

1986 Wapping dispute led to new technology and cheaper production

late 1990s all newspapers struggling to compete with online media

IT and the internet

Explosive rise of new technology from the mid 1990s:

1997 20 per cent of UK households had a mobile phone

2007 78 per cent of UK households had a mobile phone

1998 29 per cent of UK households had personal computers

2009 70 per cent of UK households had personal computers

1998 10 per cent of UK households had an internet connection

2007 61 per cent of UK households had an internet connection

2010 60 per cent of adults used the internet every day

Has national identity been changed by television and technology?

What makes people British? A common history, culture and language perhaps, and also shared values and customs. National identity suggests people have a common feeling of belonging to one country. It is a hard concept to define. It is even more difficult to judge whether the media has strengthened or weakened a sense of national identity.

Case study: Television and national identity

For many British people, the coronation of Elizabeth II in 1953 was their first experience of watching television. This occasion was a communal event; families, neighbours and friends crammed into living rooms, sharing sandwiches and drinks while they viewed the great occasion. More than ten million people watched the coronation in other people's homes. Television included people who might have been excluded by cost or distance. Later, television provided a regular audience for other national events: the Grand National in spring, Remembrance Day in November and the Queen's Christmas Day message. Patriotism was fostered by watching the nation's sports' teams in action; for instance, England's victory over Germany in the 1966 World Cup. Television programmes and films also nurtured a sense of national identity. In the 1950s and 1960s war films such as *The Dam Busters* (1955) and *The Great Escape* (1963) recreated a nostalgic pride in the spirit of those who fought in the war. Later, gentle drama and sitcoms, such as *Dad's Army* (1968–77) and *The Good Life* (1975–78), celebrated the eccentricities of the British character. Soap operas such as *Coronation Street* consistently attracted a huge audience and their plots were the talk of the bus stop, the office and the cinema queue. The regional organisation of commercial television, which arrived in 1955, led to better geographical coverage, also reflected in soaps such as *Brookside* and *Emmerdale Farm*. Soaps, especially, seem to have helped forge our national identity (see left).

> They not only reflect our identity; they are part of the cultural artefacts which construct and shape the same.
>
> (D. Hobson, *Soap Opera* (2003))

So there is a powerful argument that television has helped create a sense of national unity.

Yet this view can be challenged:

- Even the 1953 coronation was not watched on television by a majority of British people, either because they could not access a television or did not wish to do so. Those who viewed it on television may have shared a common patriotic experience but this may have created a strong sense of exclusion for those who did not see it.

- American shows such as *Dallas* and *Dynasty* were hugely popular. *Neighbours* won higher viewing figures in the UK than in its native Australia. This strengthens the view that television diluted British culture with the increasing popularity of foreign settings, and Australian or American styles, customs and language.

- The BBC was dominated by England and particularly London and the South East. Despite regional programming, the accents, programmes and topics reflected this dominance. This may have helped to create a uniform language and viewpoint but possibly undermined local culture and customs which are part of Britain's heritage.

- Some programmes challenged the cosy status quo and led to political rows – such as *The War Game* (1965) and *The Monocled Mutineer* (1986). *The War Game* gave a grim portrayal of the effects of nuclear war and was withdrawn from the BBC schedule as a result. *The Monocled Mutineer* told the story of a mutiny in the First World War, challenging the traditional view of loyal and brave soldiers in the conflict. The programme was broadcast but strongly condemned by the Conservative Party chairman at the time, Norman Tebbit. These programmes showed how television broadcasting could divide political opinion.

- Television viewing became increasingly isolated and disparate, with multiple channels and TV sets in bedrooms. In the 1950s family viewing may have been a shared experience in a darkened living room but by the late 1980s its influence may have led to people spending less time together and having fewer common experiences.

The impact of television on national unity is hard to unravel. The huge popularity of certain programmes and events made viewing a national shared experience at times. At others, it could be argued, British traditions and identity were diluted by the immense popularity of the styles, tastes and language seen in imported foreign series on the small screen. There is some evidence that a more uniform national culture was imposed by the dominance of London-based broadcasting. So-called 'BBC English' replaced local dialects. Yet this was not universally the case. The Welsh fought a strong campaign to gain and retain their own Welsh language channel, S4C, and regarded the mainstream Channel 4 as a 'foreign' alternative. Television has influenced globalisation, diversity and national identity but the nature and extent of that influence has been varied, changeable and hard to measure.

Case study: The internet and national identity

> Forty years ago, the typical person in the western world read the local newspaper. It told you which local butcher was retiring, who had celebrated their fiftieth wedding anniversary, and it covered the local politicians, athletes and business owners. Twenty years ago, the typical person read the national newspaper. It covered the national elite. Today that person gets news or Twitter feeds from websites that cover the global elite: everyone from Lady Gaga to Barack Obama.
>
> (S. Kuper, 'Now the rich are always with us' in *Financial Times* magazine, 18 June 2011)

In this passage the journalist Simon Kuper explains how the nature of news and information has been transformed by new technology. The internet supersedes national boundaries and global news stories are pushing aside national news. British legal injunctions have lost their force and the voice of the British 'man in the street' is disappearing from sight. In this new 'global village' British people are more likely to know about the fashions of American pop stars than the name of their local mayor or MP. According to this view, national unity and identity have been severely undermined by the IT revolution and the news is dominated by tales of international celebrity.

Read more about the impact of new technologies in these books:

Steve Woolgar, *Virtual Society? Technology, Cyberbole, Reality* (2002)

Dan Gillmor, *We, the Media* (2004)

Consider these questions:

1 In what ways has television created a stronger sense of national identity?

2 In what ways might it be considered a divisive influence?

3 How can it be argued that the internet has weakened a sense of national identity?

4 How have these arguments been challenged?

After answering these questions, add notes to the diagram you created at the start of this chapter.

For other writers, however, such as Dan Gillmor, the internet has been a force for democracy and inclusion. The old style media created a 'them and us' mentality with journalists lecturing their public audience. Without formal barriers of qualifications and resources, the internet has allowed many more people to have a voice through websites and blogging. Local and family history have flourished as have community associations and pressure groups with much cheaper and quicker methods of communication. Far from creating a divided society, the IT revolution has encouraged greater inclusion and engagement for a wider range of people.

Even the assumption that new technology has had a revolutionary impact has been challenged. Wide and inclusive access to the internet is a very recent development. A survey in 2000 found that a third of British adults had no intention of ever using the internet. In 1998 less than 10 per cent of British households had internet access and it was not until 2000 that this rose to more than 25 per cent. In 2001 more than 40 per cent of households had home access to the internet in London and the South East but it was less than 30 per cent in the North East, Wales and Northern Ireland. By 2010 more than 70 per cent of British households had internet connections but elderly, less educated and poorer members of society were still much less likely to be online.

Recent research has also suggested that the impact of the internet may not be as universal or dramatic as originally supposed. It has often been counter-intuitive. It is a common belief that the internet has led to more social isolation yet in many cases it has been shown to increase a sense of community and belonging. It was thought that the virtual world would replace 'real' experiences but more often, it seems, it supplements them. Online museums have led to increases in museum visits. There is also evidence that people hold on to their traditions and local contexts when they embrace new technology. Sending a colleague an email at work does not replace a chat over coffee. Steve Woolgar has summed up these findings:

> The new technologies are not being used to the extent we imagined, by the people anticipated, nor in the ways we expected.
>
> (S. Woolgar, *Virtual Society? Technology, Cyberbole, Reality* (2002))

The impact of the internet has been so extensive and so fast, it is probably too soon for historians to assess it. Not only has it affected the way people communicate, it has also changed the way the media is consumed. Clearly the internet has broken down international boundaries in many ways but how far this has resulted in a dilution of national identity remains to be seen.

How far have class barriers been broken down by film and television?

In the 1940s and 1950s British film and television had been dominated by middle-class elites: actors, producers and directors were public school educated with Oxbridge accents and conservative values. It was partly for this reason that American films were so popular and the more open-minded commercial television quickly outstripped the BBC ratings after its launch in 1955. It was difficult for anyone with a working-class background to have a career in film or television and their portrayals on screen were stereotypical. In order to assess how far this situation changed in the 1960s and onwards, closer examination of film and television's changing views of the working class will be considered.

Case study: Films of the late 1950s and 1960s and the working class

It is the 'new wave' films that appeared to challenge the British class system. The release of *Room at the Top* in 1959 featuring Joe Lampton, a young man happy to break the rules in order to rise from his working-class roots, broke new ground. Arthur Seaton in *Saturday Night, Sunday Morning* (1960) had no time for social conventions; he slept with another man's wife, got drunk, was offensive and showed no respect for his factory supervisor. These so-called 'kitchen sink' dramas challenged the values and assumptions of the middle classes with much more realistic and gritty views of everyday life. The films have a strong tone of negativity and hostility towards the new affluence, materialism and the growing dominance of a uniform mass media. In *A Kind of Loving* the vile mother-in-law was addicted to TV quiz shows and Arthur Seaton in *Saturday Night, Sunday Morning* expressed contempt for his fellow workers who were content as long as they had their fags and telly. In this the new wave films reflected the views of contemporary writers such as Hoggart who mourned the loss of the supposedly supportive pre-war working-class culture. Yet new wave films offered no solutions to working-class problems and focused almost exclusively on the individual, leading male's viewpoint. Films of the 1940s and 1950s, such as the Ealing comedies and wartime dramas, portrayed communities working together; the new wave films showed young men seeking pleasure through sex, drink and money. It could be argued that these films themselves reflected the decline in the class consciousness of the working class.

No one would claim the *Carry On* films presented any serious kind of challenge to the British class system in the 1960s. The unadventurous storylines were so predictable that the film expert Jeffrey Richards has commented that the 29 *Carry On* films were the same film made 29 times. The humour in the series was firmly rooted in traditional working-class jokes, to be seen in saucy seaside postcards or in the pre-war music hall. *Carry On* continued the chirpy cheekiness seen in the 1930s film stars George Formby and Gracie Fields, both from working-class Lancashire backgrounds. Figures of authority were the object of mickey-taking: matrons, police officers, head teachers and factory bosses were depicted

cockney
From the East End of
London, traditionally a
working-class area

as pompous and unsympathetic compared to those they were ordering about. The writer of the first six films, Norman Hudis, and many of the actors, such as Barbara Windsor, had a **cockney** background themselves. The films' ability to tap into these established strands of working-class humour was hugely successful throughout the decade. It is significant that when the scriptwriters strayed from this format, in *Carry On at Your Convenience* (1971), featuring a trouble-making trade unionist in a toilet factory, the film flopped.

How far did these films influence attitudes to class in British society? The new wave films addressed working-class life more directly and frankly than ever before. Regional accents and urban industrial settings highlighted this deliberate choice. A specialist cinema magazine predicted in 1960 that *Saturday Night, Sunday Morning* would appeal to '**class cinemas** (for the quality of its production) and **industrial halls** (for its identifiable truth about working-class life)'. And this was true; both *Saturday Night* and *Room at the Top* were box office successes. Yet the impact of new wave was, in the end, fairly marginal and short lived. The peak of their success was from 1959 to 1963 and they were only a small proportion of the films produced. *Carry On* films represented a much more enduring and popular taste in working-class cinema, going with stereotypical views of class and society. In these years of declining cinema audiences, it is likely that both *Carry On* and new wave reflected more than changed the social attitudes of their audiences. In the case of new wave, however, social issues such as class mobility were firmly put on the public agenda.

class cinemas
Middle-class cinemas,
where more 'arty' kinds
of films were shown
industrial halls
Cinemas in working-class
areas

Case study: Television and the working class

'We reject the view', the Pilkington Report on Broadcasting stated firmly in 1962, 'that television "will be shaped by society".' Rather, they went on to argue, programme makers themselves help to mould that society. This is a chicken and egg kind of question. Television has had to reflect key changes in society but few would dispute that it has also helped to make those changes too. Average television viewing hours have grown steadily since the 1950s, levelling out at three to four hours a day in the twenty-first century. Even in the 1980s three-quarters of British adults were regularly watching a television soap opera that usually focused on the daily lives of working-class families. It seems probable that these programmes both reflected and helped to mould the image of the British working class.

Recent critics such as Phil Redmond and Owen Jones have attacked negative television portrayals of the working class in such series as *The Royle Family*, *Shameless* and *Little Britain*. They have suggested that the writers and producers, who are mostly middle-class themselves, have created a view of the working classes as lazy, irresponsible and unattractive in the minds of television viewers. Their attack is a little unfair as the series show warmth and affection in both the characters themselves and their relationships. Nor are the writers and actors of *The Royle Family* uniformly middle class: Caroline Aherne is the daughter of an Irish railway worker and Ricky Tomlinson has radical working-class roots. Despite this, these programmes may reinforce negative working-class stereotypes. A survey of 2006 showed that 70 per cent of television professionals thought that the slovenly teenage mother, Vicky Pollard, in the *Little Britain* series was an accurate portrayal of the white working class, confirming the view of Jones and Redmond that these series have strengthened negative working-class stereotypes.

This has been contrasted with some more positive images in television series in previous decades where working-class characters might be flawed, but are nearly always sympathetic. Below is a summary of some earlier, very popular, programmes that featured working-class life. In these series there are working-class characters who are anxious to better themselves and to do the best they can for their families. Arguably they are depicted in a more sympathetic and attractive light than later series, such as *The Royle Family*. There is some evidence, for instance, that *Boys from the Blackstuff* raised sympathy for the thousands of jobless in cities like Liverpool at the height of unemployment in the early 1980s. These series made the working class more real and visible to many television viewers, with a range of regional settings and accents, presenting a contrast to the middle-class dramas that preceded them. It is probable that these earlier programmes led to greater acceptance and understanding of working-class life yet they may also have strengthened stereotypical views such as the 'loveable rogue' or the 'feckless youth'.

Steptoe and Son (1960s and 1970s)

Albert Steptoe and his son Harold had a **rag and bone** business. Harold gets exasperated with his father and is always trying to improve himself and the business.

rag and bone
A business that involved trading in junk, i.e. low quality clothes, furniture and materials that people had thrown out or sold cheaply

---

The Likely Lads (1964–66)

This comedy drama series featured two working-class lads in the North East using their earnings to enjoy sport, drinking and girls. They fall into various scrapes with the humour relying on the contrast between the more serious and ambitious Terry, and the more laid-back Bob.

Boys from the Blackstuff (1982)

This followed the fortunes of five unemployed men in Liverpool struggling in the recession. Yosser Hughes battled with police and authorities to keep his family together, all the time searching for work with the memorable catchphrase 'Gizza job' (Give us a job).

Only Fools and Horses (1981–91, specials until 2003)

The Trotter brothers run a market stall in South London, always dreaming of making a fortune in their trade of dodgy and black market goods. Their plans nearly always end up going wrong.

Television's impact on class relations goes beyond the screen depictions of the working class. Some series have directly addressed social tensions. In the first episode of *Coronation Street* shown in 1960, the son returned from college with new habits and ideas that were resented by his traditional working-class dad. Comedies such as *Keeping Up Appearances*, *Fawlty Towers* and *Are You Being Served?* made fun of snobbery and social differences. It is hard to gauge how far they challenged these attitudes but from the 1990s such themes have been less visible and less topical. Other social issues such as sexism and racism seem to have replaced the British obsession with class. Some writers have suggested that this reflects changes in British society itself.

> By the late 1990s, the working class were no longer a working class
> – their traditions, habits, jobs, even in some places their speech,
> were given over to new forms of transcendence offered by celebrity
> culture and credit cards and the bogus life of the fantasy rich …
>
> (A. O'Hagan, 'The Age of Indifference',
> *The Guardian*, 10 January 2009)

Television viewing habits have also reflected social differences. The advent of ITV in 1955 led many working-class families to switch from the stuffy BBC to the more entertaining quiz shows, American imports and soap operas offered by commercial television. The Pilkington Committee (1962), dominated by members of the establishment, condemned the triviality of much of this popular ITV programming. The notion that shared television viewing broke down social barriers is weakened by the evidence that the middle and working classes seemed to be watching different channels. Yet, arguably, television itself has created this consumerist society where material goods, celebrity and a chance of fame have undermined a sense of social class. By 2008 shows such as *The X Factor* and *Britain's Got Talent* were beating *Coronation Street* in the ratings. Soap operas, watched by an estimated third of the population, focus on individuals and incidents, with heroes and villains from different social backgrounds. Since the 1990 Broadcasting Act there has been a huge expansion of channels provided through cable and satellite, leading to a greater diversification of audiences. New technologies from VCRs in the 1980s to the huge range of choices for recording and viewing in the twenty-first century, allow individuals to view whatever they want, whenever they want.

These two case studies show just how difficult it is to assess the impact of the media on society. At the same time that television and film were evolving, so was the structure of British society. The confidence of the Pilkington Committee that media makers could shape society seems misplaced. Clearly, there was a complex interplay between film, television and society. This certainly applies to the portrayal and involvement of the working class in the visual media.

Consider these questions:

1. In what ways have film and television presented the working class more realistically since the 1950s?

2. Write down several ways in which the working class have been presented favourably and several ways in which they have been presented unfavourably in film and television.

3. How have film and television helped or hindered social unity in the UK?

4. Note down any ways in which television might have created a society more concerned with consumerism than class.

After answering these questions, add notes to the diagram you created at the start of this chapter which highlight ways that film and television increased or decreased social harmony in Britain.

Was the decline in deference due to the media?

The permissive society

It was in the 1960s that most believe the permissive society was born. Censorship was relaxed, suicide was no longer a crime, murderers were not killed, homosexuality was tolerated, divorce became accessible and women could get the pill. Liberals celebrated the increased personal freedom, the flowering of the arts and the end of 'stuffiness'. Conservatives deplored the lowering of moral standards, the lack of inhibition and the foul language and sexual daring of press and screen. Modern historians debate how far and how fast permissiveness arrived in the 1960s decade. But there is agreement that the decade marks the beginning of the end of legal and moral restraints on personal and private behaviour.

It is very hard to judge what causes changes in moral attitudes but the following reasons have been suggested:

- the decline in organised religion and the secularisation of society
- multi-culturalism
- the weakening of the family unit and the increase in divorce
- a legal culture of rights rather than responsibilities
- the growth of commerce and celebrity culture
- the impact of technology and the media.

No one would deny that television has had a huge influence in moulding modern British society but the nature of that influence is hard to judge. Certainly in the 1960s and 1970s, television programmes eroded the culture of 'deference' which had existed before. In the 1950s people in authority, whether they were teachers, policemen or park keepers, were treated with respect. Institutions such as the monarchy and the Church of England were uncritically revered. The class system still held sway, working men often doffed their caps and addressed their superiors as 'sir'. These habits disappeared in subsequent decades. Publications like *Private Eye*, new wave films like *Room at the Top* and theatre shows such as *Beyond the Fringe* went some way to challenge the old values. But television satire had far more impact.

Case study: *That Was The Week That Was (TW3)*

TW3 ran from 1962 to 1963, pushing the limits of acceptability and leading to numerous complaints. It was started with the encouragement of the liberal Director General of the BBC, Hugh Greene, who wanted to 'prick the pomposity of public figures'. One of its more controversial episodes was the 'Consumers' Guide to Religions', when different faiths were treated like goods in shops. It dared to poke fun at leading politicians, and even the Queen. In December 1962 the BBC Director General drafted a letter of apology to the current Prime Minister, Harold Macmillan, fearing the programme had gone too far. In response to the same programme, Macmillan sent a note saying that no action should be taken against the

Personal story

In school assembly when I was growing up, we would cheerfully sing this verse of the hymn 'All things bright and beautiful':
'The rich man in his castle
the poor man at his gate
God made them high and lowly
And ordered their Estate.'
A clear message to accept one's place in society.

broadcaster as it was better to be laughed at than ignored. According to the leading Conservative, Ted Heath, *TW3* was responsible for the 'death of deference'. Immensely popular, it regularly attracted a late night audience of 12 million. It was dropped in 1964, supposedly because it was too controversial to coincide with a general election.

Even the satirists themselves, however, were sceptical about the extent of their influence. One of the creators of the 1980s hit show *Spitting Image*, which poked fun at Margaret Thatcher and John Major among others, stated that the series 'achieved nothing except it possibly made the government slightly more powerful than when we had found it'. Many have discounted claims that *TW3* helped the Labour Party to victory in 1964 yet most would accept that it created a more openly critical attitude to those in authority, especially among the young.

In his role as Director General of the BBC in the 1960s, Hugh Greene was keen to challenge the dull conservatism of his predecessors. In 1966 the drama documentary *Cathy Come Home* shocked viewers with its realistic portrayal of a young, homeless family. The racy police series *Z Cars* was set on a modern estate, featuring issues such as domestic abuse and drugs, in contrast to its homely predecessor *Dixon of Dock Green*. Challenging television programmes fitted in with Greene's view of the role of television:

> I believe we have a duty to take account of the changes in society, to be ahead of public opinion rather than always to wait upon it. I believe that great broadcasting organisations, with their immense powers of patronage for writers and artists, should not neglect to cultivate young writers who may, by many, be considered 'shocking'.

Greene's liberal approach to television broadcasting certainly had its critics. Lord Reith, who had dominated the BBC in the pre-war years, wrote that Greene:

> ... follows the mob in every disgusting manifestation of the age ... the BBC is no longer on the Lord's side.

That was a view that was firmly endorsed by one determined campaigner: Mary Whitehouse, whose impact you will read about on page 107.

It is worth learning and understanding these key terms:

iconoclasm **permissive society** hedonism **moral relativism** **individualism** secularisation **pluralism** openness decline in deference **new morality**

Story of two princesses

The decline in deference applied even to the royal family. Treated with loyalty and respect in the 1950s and 1960s, by the 1980s public interest was such that royal family members were regarded as 'fair game' with little chance of privacy.

Snapshot 1: Photo that was not published

Queen Elizabeth's coronation day in June 1953 was one of the biggest media events of the century. Naturally, her younger sister, Princess Margaret, played a significant role. When waiting at the church entrance, Margaret gazed up at her companion, Group Captain Peter Townsend, and flicked a bit of fluff from his uniform. It was an innocent, yet telling, gesture and was noticed by a tabloid news photographer. But Townsend was a divorcee, a much older man and, in everyone's view, a wholly unsuitable partner for a princess. The revelation of this relationship would have been dynamite. Loyalty and restraint meant the image was never seen: we can't even publish it here.

△ Princess Margaret and Peter Townsend leaving Windsor Castle, 12 April 1952.

Snapshot 2: Photo that was published

In February 1982 Prince Charles and a pregnant Diana went on holiday to the Bahamas. They were tracked down by determined press photographers, who used long lenses to capture pictures of the bikini-clad Princess. The images were in the tabloids the next day. The royal family were disgusted at this invasion of privacy, the Queen calling it 'the blackest day in the history of British journalism'. *The Sun* newspaper's apology was put adjacent to another photo of Diana on the beach. These photos are not available for licence any more.

△ Princess Diana is hounded by the press after leaving a restaurant in London, 1994.

Consider these questions:

1 How has the media contributed to the decline in deference? Write down some examples.

2 In what ways did the media create greater disagreement about moral and social issues?

After answering these questions, add notes to the diagram you created at the start of this chapter.

The problem, though, is that the age of deference has swung to the other extreme of the age of cynicism, with large sections of society holding all authority in contempt.

(A. Browne, *Has there been a decline in values in British society?*, Joseph Rowntree Foundation, 2008)

The Profumo affair

JULY 1961 CHRISTINE KEELER IS INTRODUCED TO JOHN PROFUMO, SECRETARY OF STATE FOR WAR, BY HER MANAGER STEPHEN WARD AT LORD ASTOR'S COUNTRY MANSION. THE GUESTS ARE INVITED TO BATHE IN THE NUDE.

PROFUMO IS STRUCK BY KEELER'S BEAUTY, AND THE COUPLE START A PASSIONATE AFFAIR.

MEANWHILE KEELER IS ALSO HAVING AN AFFAIR WITH EUGENE IVANOV, A NAVAL ATTACHÉ AT THE RUSSIAN EMBASSY.

MARCH 1963 RUMOURS OF HIS AFFAIR FORCE PROFUMO TO MAKE A PUBLIC STATEMENT IN THE HOUSE OF COMMONS. HE STATES THAT THERE WAS NO 'IMPROPRIETY' IN HIS RELATIONSHIP WITH KEELER.

STEPHEN WARD IS ARRESTED FOR LIVING OFF IMMORAL EARNINGS AND MORE DETAILS OF THE AFFAIR START TO LEAK.

JUNE 1963 PROFUMO RESIGNS AND MAKES A PUBLIC APOLOGY, ADMITTING THAT HE LIED TO THE HOUSE OF COMMONS.

AUGUST 1963 STEPHEN WARD IS FOUND DEAD FROM AN OVERDOSE ON THE LAST DAY OF HIS TRIAL.

SEPTEMBER 1963 AN OFFICIAL REPORT BY LORD DENNING CONCLUDES THAT NATIONAL SECURITY HAD NOT BEEN PUT AT RISK BY THE SCANDAL.

LORD DENNING'S REPORT

Public manners and private morals: did Mary speak for the majority?

According to Mary Whitehouse, a Shropshire schoolteacher, 'homosexuality, prostitution and sexual intercourse' became the routine topic of conversation at family mealtimes and in school playgrounds in the summer of 1963. Why? Because the Profumo affair was the top news story on television and national newspapers.

The Profumo affair had serious political and diplomatic repercussions happening, as it did, at the height of the **Cold War**. But it also changed the reticence of the British media when it came to the sexual affairs of the elites. Profumo had threatened legal action against the press so when his deception was revealed, the newspapers did not hold back. Christine Keeler commented: 'They wanted to hear about the sex, of course, but not the rest; no one wanted to hear the rest.' Revelations of immoral goings on in high society also weakened their social superiority. When Christine Keeler's friend and fellow call girl, Mandy Rice Davies, was called to the witness box she was told that Lord Astor's version of events differed from hers. Her answer 'He would say that, wouldn't he?' and the resulting laughter symbolised a real change in social attitudes.

Details of the scandal were openly described in the press to the disgust of people like Mrs Whitehouse. Keeler sold her story to the *News of the World* for more than £20,000, a small fortune in those days. More explicit coverage of sex stories was followed by more overt images, such as *The Sun's* inclusion of a topless page 3 pin-up from 1970.

Mary Whitehouse and the permissive society

Mary Whitehouse was shocked by the influence of the media on her teenage pupils. A committed Christian, she felt that traditional values were being continually undermined by foul language, violent behaviour and sexual misconduct. In 1964 she set up the 'Clean Up TV campaign' and started an unrelenting fight to restore what she called 'a sense of values'. She soon became an object of ridicule: the Director General of the BBC had a painting of her in his office with five breasts and there was even a spoof television series based on her activities. Leaders of the media and the arts were quick to condemn her as narrow-minded and out of touch.

> The whole difficulty with Mary Whitehouse and her movement is that they have invented a scale of values which operate for and in her group but which neither apply nor can be applied to the outside world.
> (A. Smith, documentary producer, in M. Caulfield, *Mary Whitehouse* (1976))

Mrs Whitehouse may not have spoken for a majority but she certainly spoke for many. More than 30 coaches came from all areas of the country to attend her first major meeting at Birmingham Town Hall in 1964. Her manifesto protesting against 'low standards' in television, presented to Parliament in 1965, was signed by more than 360,000 people. She won support not only from the Churches and Conservative politicians, but also from many ordinary families disturbed by the liberalisation of the media. A national opinion poll of 1970 showed that most British people at that time disapproved of nude women, dirty books, free love or the use of drugs, so her claim to speak for the man or woman in the street may not have been unfounded.

Cold War
A period of serious tensions between the Communist Soviet Union and Western countries such as the UK and the USA. In January 1963 Britain had been shaken by the revelation that Communist spies such as Kim Philby had infiltrated the British secret service

'Oh what have you done?' said Christine.

'You've disrupted the Party machine;

To lie in the nude is not very rude,

But to lie in the House is obscene.'

(A popular limerick of the time)

Among the children's programmes Mary Whitehouse objected to were *Pinky and Perky*, *Tom and Jerry* and *Dr Who*. She described *Doctor Who* as 'teatime brutality for tots'.

Lady Chatterley case

D.H. Lawrence's novel, *Lady Chatterley's Lover*, had been banned in Britain because of its explicit sexual content. In 1960 Penguin challenged the law and a case was brought against them under the Obscene Publications Act. The case attracted strong media interest with many people regarding it as a clash between the conservative elite and the rest of society. This view was confirmed when the chief prosecutor asked in court if this was a book 'you would wish your wife or servants to read'. Penguin won the case and 200,000 copies were sold in the following few days.

She had some successes: in 1971 she prosecuted the writers of the *Little Red Schoolbook* which advocated a charter of children's rights, including sex and drugs. She helped to restrict the display of pornographic material in shops. Six years later she brought a private prosecution against *Gay News* for blasphemous libel, and won. The National Viewers and Listeners Association, led by Whitehouse, became an influential pressure group, requiring television executives to consider programme content, give warnings and broadcast at appropriate times.

The struggle over the 'permissive society' in the 1960s and 1970s has often been described as a battle between conservative Christian moralists on one side, and the liberal leaders of the arts and media on the other. Whitehouse and her adherents were accused of wanting to put the clock back. Their opponents were accused of lowering moral standards. But the conflicts over censorship and morality were more complicated than that. Richard Hoggart, for instance, was a witness for book publisher Penguin in the **Lady Chatterley case**, yet deplored many aspects of the new popular culture. Many of the BBC's Board of Governors shared some of Whitehouse's concerns, for instance, about satirical shows such as *That Was The Week That Was*. The Women's Liberation movement also objected to the growth of pornography. But the wide range of Whitehouse's enemies – atheists, homosexuals, communists and feminists – antagonised potential friends. Increasingly her cause was marginalised and weakened. Even the political power of sympathisers, such as Margaret Thatcher in the 1980s, could not restore the restraint and censorship of earlier years.

Consider these questions:

1 In the Profumo affair, how did the media contribute to the declining respect for the political and social elite?

2 What were the main causes of disagreement between Mary Whitehouse and her supporters and the providers of news and entertainment in the 1960s?

After answering these questions, add notes to the diagram you created at the start of this chapter about how far the media caused a clash in moral and social values.

Has the media made Britain more racist?

One day in the autumn of 1968, Lionel Morrison, a young journalist, arrived at the offices of a leading newspaper for a job interview. He had good qualifications for the post: a degree and experience of working in many different countries. The receptionist telephoned the relevant editor who arrived in the foyer. The editor looked around but then turned to the receptionist and asked where the applicant was. Mr Morrison is black, and that, it seems, was enough to make him an impossible candidate for the job. The subsequent interview appeared to go well but he was not offered employment. A further 150 job applications over the next ten years failed, mainly, he believes, because of his colour.

By 2011 Morrison could look back on a highly distinguished career in journalism. He was the first black president of the National Union of Journalists and his work was recognised in 2000 with the award of an OBE. Yet in a speech to the NUJ in 2011 he pointed out the persistently low proportion of black people in the media – even in the NUJ itself this stood at only 2.6 per cent.

This is not only true of the print media. Talking to *The Guardian* in 2008, Lenny Henry, the black comedian, commented:

> The status quo is predominantly white and middle class. And if you're not that, well. Go to any meeting or go to any production company, you might have a black person on reception and an Asian person in IT or something. And that's it. That's appalling. What's going on?

The logical conclusion might be that the British media has always been mostly white and mostly racist. But there have been undeniable changes. The racist words 'coon' and 'nig-nog' were regularly used in one hit comedy series in the 1960s, language that has become unacceptable in the last 30 years. By 1983 the BBC had three black female news presenters. At the cinema, the 1985 film *My Beautiful Laundrette*, with its controversial story of a gay inter-racial relationship, won many awards. Black and Asian faces have been regularly seen in children's programmes and in drama series since the 1990s. On the radio and in the papers, ethnic minorities are much better represented and there are more programmes, magazines and journals aimed at their interests. A study of media reporting in the years 1996–97 found that the British media mostly adopted an anti-racist stance and presented a positive view of multi-culturalism and ethnic minorities, although this was not so true of tabloid newspapers whose reporting of these issues was 33 per cent negative.

Lenny Henry has become one of the most successful and popular black faces in the British media. How far his skin colour has affected his career is hard to assess. Early on, he drew attention to it, using colour as a tool for humour and caricature. His success has surely contributed to a far greater acceptance of black faces on screen and he has been a positive role model for many aspiring black actors, presenters and comedians. Maybe the most significant development of his career, however, has been his more recent work where race and colour have had little relevance. His varied and active media career does reflect, in many ways, the media's changing relationship with racial minorities.

Lenny Henry, racism and the media

1970s	Lenny Henry was a young engineering apprentice from the Midlands whose career was launched with his imitation of the white comedian Michael Crawford in the show *New Faces* (similar to *Britain's Got Talent*).
	Henry then joined the *Black and White Minstrel Show,* a highly popular variety show of song and dance numbers which won an international award in 1961. The other performers were 'blacked up' and their portrayal of stereotypical black singers has since been regarded as racist.
	In this early stage in his career, Henry sometimes used his colour as humour, for instance, threatening hecklers that he would move in next door to them.
1976–77	He appeared in *The Fosters*, the first British sitcom with a black cast.
1980s	Henry featured in various comedy shows, such as the children's show *Tiswas*.
1984–2004	Henry had his own show. His most popular creations for the show were Delbert Wilkins, a streetwise, pirate disc jockey, and Theophilus P. Wildebeeste, an overweight soul singer. Topical issues, such as police harassment, were raised but mostly in a light-hearted way. These impersonations were celebrated by some as lively and witty portrayals of black characters but have also been criticised for reinforcing silly stereotypical views of the black community.
	He married the white British comedian Dawn French in 1984, the celebrity couple becoming role models for successful mixed-race marriages.
1988	Henry earned substantial funds from TV commercials for Abbey National Building Society and Alpen Muesli (a breakfast cereal), confirming his popularity with the public.
1988	Henry started his long association with Comic Relief with a tour of Ethiopia. Since that time he has played a major role in this media fund-raising event.
1990s	Henry played the main role in *Chef*, a sitcom about a restaurant. The lead character just happened to be black and there was no reference to racial issues in the series.
2000s	Henry's work diversified to include acting Shakespeare's leading black character, Othello, on stage, a documentary series on British humour and a new sketch show called *Lenny Henry in Pieces*.

How far the media has achieved real racial equality in the last 30 years is controversial. Most agree that high profile presenters and reporters like Trevor McDonald and George Alagiah have acted as positive role models. Yet some say this is tokenism: presenting a black face on screen hides the fact that the key decisions off screen are overwhelmingly made by whites. Although the first black BBC governor was appointed in 1969, in 2002 all the members of the BBC executive board were white.

The relationship between the media and racial attitudes is hard to define. In the 1970s an academic researcher wrote that:

> … television drama all too often reflects and reinforces the prejudices of white Britain.
>
> (C. Husband, *White Media and Black Britain: a critical look at the role of the media in race relations today* (1975))

In the twenty-first century few would make such a strong claim. Yet well-intentioned television writers and producers often stumble when trying to address this contentious issue as these two examples confirm:

Till Death Do Us Part

In the 1960s and 1970s the series *Till Death Do Us Part* was one of the most popular comedies on the BBC. It featured Alf Garnett, a working-class East Ender, as its main character. Garnett dominated the programmes with his vicious and prejudiced attacks on those around him and larger national issues. Many of these speeches were racist and new immigrants were presented as a threat to traditional working-class life. Both Warren Mitchell, who played Garnett, and Johnny Speight, who wrote the series, wanted to expose these views as offensive and stupid. Yet many in the audience laughed with Garnett rather than at him. Research in 1972 showed that most regarded him as a loveable buffoon and that he endorsed (though did not necessarily strengthen) the intolerant attitudes of the viewers.

EastEnders

EastEnders, the BBC's leading soap, has had black and Asian characters in its cast since it started in the 1980s. In this series ethnic minority actors have been doctors and health visitors, not confined to lower status jobs, and racial issues such as mixed-race relationships have been tackled head on. In 2009 an all-black episode was broadcast, telling the story of two black families' experiences of living in Britain since the 1950s. The older characters described the racism they had suffered and the ill treatment of black people in the Notting Hill race riots of 1958. The reaction was mixed, with the BBC receiving nearly 250 complaints.

Here are some of the comments on the all-black *EastEnders* episode on one newspaper website:

> It's good to see the BBC finally starting to accurately portray the demographic reality of London in their propaganda programs/'soaps' nowadays.
>
> (draeghalore)

> The BBC really have no flaming idea – if they'd have had a more diverse cast 20 years ago then they wouldn't have had to make such a ruddy song and dance over having an all-black cast episode. I'm black – and I found it a pathetic attempt by the BBC, who haven't got the faintest idea about how to handle diversity in the first place.
>
> (MissyMR)

That the British media has become far more diverse and inclusive in the past 50 years is undeniable. In television, in particular, there has been much more recognition of racial issues and greater variety in personnel. Changes in the press have been more marginal, with the tabloids rather slow to recruit ethnic minority journalists and continuing an anti-immigration stance, which some regard as racist.

When questioned in 2006, 21 per cent of ethnic minority respondents believed that there was still racism in the print media.

Note down evidence that the media increased or decreased racial divisions in society and add them to your diagram. Use the following prompts to help you:

1 How far have ethnic minorities been presented in positive ways in the media?

2 How far have racial minorities had a fair chance to work in the media?

3 How far has the raising of racial issues in the media improved race relations?

For each of the above, think about the broadcast media and the press and note differences between them.

Review: Has the British media been a unifying force?

The Queen's Coronation 1953

It was good to be English. Those feelings have lasted for the last 50 years.

(Vivian Draper, who watched the Coronation as a child)

20.4 million people watched the event on television.

Death of Princess Diana 1997

I always believed that the press would kill her in the end. But not even I could imagine that they would take such a direct hand in her death as seems to be the case.

(Earl Spencer, Princess Diana's brother, 1997)

32 million people watched the funeral service on British televisions.

This chapter has highlighted the complexity of the relationship between media and society. There are no reliable methods of measuring the impact of the media on British people's lives just as there is no simple way of estimating how the media has adjusted to social change. There are moments when the media appears to have been a unifying force; sharing national emotions at royal events, sporting triumphs and disasters and when the nation is at war. But there have also been times when entertainers and reporters have been prejudiced, divisive and ill informed. The amazing pace of change in the media also presents huge difficulties in assessing its impact.

Furthermore, changes in the media have coincided with other changes in British society, which have also shifted social attitudes and values. Rising living standards and increasing consumerism have led to less obvious differences in dress, language and behaviour. Levi jeans and Marks and Spencer underwear are happily worn by people of different ages, classes and cultures. Longer years in secondary school and widening opportunities at higher education have further eroded class barriers. In the past, sport and music had opened up opportunities for the working class to 'better themselves' as the 1930s careers of the Welsh boxer Tommy Farr and the singer Gracie Fields confirm.

Marriage of Prince William and Kate Middleton 2011

... a chance [to] ... celebrate the great things about our country.

(Prime Minister David Cameron)

The royal wedding was watched by 26 million people in UK homes.

In the post-war years, more routes out of poverty were created. The media has played a part in this process alongside other factors; the most recent creation of 'reality TV stars' such as Jade Goody being a notable example.

When I was growing up the family television was a small and rather fuzzy grey screen that gradually disappeared into a little dot when turned off. My family acquired its first colour television when I was a teenager but when I left home there were still only three channels broadcasting. We listened to Radio 4 in the mornings and my older sisters sometimes tuned in to Radio 1. *The Times* was delivered daily; a broadsheet predictable in content and layout. In my children's lives, the rate of change has been phenomenal. The number of television channels has multiplied, newspapers have become bulky, colourful and diverse, and commercial radio has challenged BBC dominance. Yet it is new technology, especially computers, which has transformed my children's lives.

Radio, television and newspapers can now be accessed online with innumerable opportunities for consumers to choose their consumption and feed back their tastes. It is, perhaps, too early to assess the social influence of these changes although some, such as increasing obesity, are becoming apparent. Computer technology can be blamed for the increasing social fragmentation of society, with individuals sitting in front of screens instead of interacting face to face. Yet it has also multiplied the number of social interactions, given an online voice to those who were rarely heard before, and provided a means of challenging our cultural and political leaders. Whether this massive increase in access to news and information and in mass communications and interactions will make the British more united or divided is, as yet, impossible to decide.

Reading over this section, review how far the media has been a divisive or unifying force in British society by studying your annotated diagram. In this chapter, more than any other, you will have to use the provided evidence to put forward supported theories rather than clear judgements.

Here are some suggestions to help you. Find evidence from the chapter and your annotated diagram to support or refute them:

1 The British media has been a unifying influence in the past 60 years, making people feel a stronger sense of national identity.

2 The media has helped to break down class barriers and create a more equal and harmonious society.

3 Social attitudes have been liberalised by the media, leading to greater tolerance and less censorship.

4 Race relations have been improved by the media, breaking down prejudice and leading to more racial equality.

The media, class and celebrity (1)

It has sometimes been suggested that the media has replaced respect for the higher social classes and admiration of the monarchy with worship of celebrities and film stars. This is an inaccurate generalisation. Hollywood stars have been admired since the 1920s with popular magazines such as *Picturegoer* achieving mass sales in the inter-war years. At the same time, interest in the royal family has remained remarkably consistent. *Hello!* magazine has colour features on minor royals and aristocratic families alongside stories of newly created stars of reality television. Nor is the television personality a new phenomenon, as the story of Gilbert Harding below suggests:

workhouses
Institutions for poor people who could not support themselves

Gilbert Harding: a television personality of the 1950s

Gilbert Harding was an unlikely television star in many ways. Overweight and not good looking, he was the son of the master and matron of a Hereford **workhouse**. In the 1930s he had worked as a teacher and policeman before becoming a journalist. After presenting various programmes on the radio, in the 1950s Harding started his television career.

△ Gilbert Harding (right) and the *What's My Line?* panel.

114

In these early days of television, quiz shows were very popular and Gilbert Harding was a regular on *What's My Line?* where panellists had to guess the job of the contestant. Harding made few concessions to the new medium, and did not feel the need to tone down his brusque personality when on screen. In 1952 he told a particularly evasive contestant 'I am tired of looking at you', the rudeness of this comment causing large numbers of complaints to the BBC and criticism in the national press the following day. Instead of ending his career, Harding's insults added to his appeal and the programme's ratings – a massive 12 million viewers at its peak. Similar to Anne Robinson many years later on *The Weakest Link*, Harding made fun of people's names or their home towns. His television fame expanded his career and opportunities; he introduced various other television programmes, wrote regular newspaper columns, published a book on manners and earned large sums from advertising. Recognised wherever he went, Harding's daily exploits, whether illnesses, railway trips or quarrels in cafes, regularly hit the headlines. He was, perhaps, Britain's first real media personality and certainly the most famous television star of the decade.

Behind this career success, however, there was a lonely and frustrated man. Harding was a homosexual who had to keep his sexuality secret. He had a problem with alcohol and often appeared slightly drunk for his numerous television performances. He had always aspired to work on serious programmes but ended up in light entertainment. In a *Face to Face* interview in 1960, he broke down in tears under the intensive questioning. Some have attributed this to the recent death of his mother; others to the probing hints about his sexuality. Either way, Harding died of an asthma attack only a few months later, still in his early fifties.

Aspects of Harding's story reveal stark changes in the media over the last 60 years. In the twenty-first century his sexuality and alcoholism would certainly have been exposed. But his career also demonstrates the long-term roots of the current celebrity culture. Even in the 1950s, stories of television stars were reported in the national press. Their private lives were the source of public scrutiny and interest. For the stars themselves, fame brought money and opportunity, with loss of privacy and personal freedom as the price.

Homosexual relationships were illegal in the 1950s.

The media, class and celebrity (2)

Bob Boothby: political scandal and the media

Robert Boothby was a Conservative politician who had a long and distinguished parliamentary career. Educated at Eton, he became an MP in his twenties and served in the Ministry of Food in Churchill's wartime government. He was knighted in 1953 and created Baron Boothby in 1958. He combined his political activities with writing and appearances on radio and television where his ready wit made him a popular guest. A highly sociable man, he had many friends among the rich and famous.

Boothby's private life was controversial to say the least. In 1929 he started an affair with Dorothy Macmillan, a passionate relationship which lasted until her death in 1966. She was the wife of his fellow conservative Harold Macmillan, who became Prime Minister in 1957. The couple were frequently seen together, shared holidays and, at times, openly lived together. Many believed that Dorothy's daughter, Sarah, born in 1930, was Boothby's child. Their relationship was well known in political and aristocratic circles but was never mentioned in the press.

Boothby's affair did not prevent him from marrying. His short-lived marriage to Diana Cavendish in 1935 ended in divorce only a few months later. This was still shocking at this time and Boothby wrote to the media baron Lord Beaverbrook:

> I realise that there must be a good deal of publicity. But don't let your boys hunt me down. Because I am not going to let go of public life; and still believe that one day I may do something.

Boothby was lucky to hold on to his Scottish seat, despite this, and in the long term his political prospects were not greatly damaged.

Further scandal touched Boothby in 1964. The *Sunday Mirror* printed a story under the headline 'Peer and a Gangster: Yard Probe Public Men at Seaside Parties' alleging a homosexual affair between a lord who was a 'household name' and a leading East End criminal who was being investigated by the police. Although no names were provided, it was easy to guess that the peer was Boothby and the

△ Front page of the *Sunday Mirror*, 19 July 1964.

gangster, the notorious Ronnie Kray. It seems, however, that the paper had little hard evidence to go on except for a photograph of Boothby with Kray, sitting together on a sofa at Boothby's London home. Boothby quickly denied the allegations, writing in a letter to *The Times*: 'I have never been to all-male parties in Mayfair. I have met the man alleged to be King of the Underworld (Ron Kray) only three times, on business matters. I am not, and never have been, homosexual.'

In the aftermath of the Profumo affair, it seems that both the Conservative and Labour party leaders were keen to hush up any kind of sexual scandal. The police denied any investigation into Boothby, although a criminal case was brought against the Krays in the following year. Boothby employed powerful lawyers and the frightened editor of the *Mirror* soon settled the issue with an abject apology and the huge sum of £40,000 as compensation.

△ Robert Boothby (right) with Reginald Kray.

Even now the complete truth of this episode cannot be established for certain. New evidence suggests that Boothby had regular contacts with the Krays for well over a year, not just the three businesslike meetings he claimed. Photographs of Boothby at shady gambling clubs in the company of known rent boys raise questions about his sexual behaviour. He certainly attended London parties in the company of the Labour MP, Tom Driberg, who was a known homosexual. So although Robert Rhodes James, in his biography of Boothby in 1991, refuted all the allegations, it is hard to believe Boothby's complete denial.

What does Boothby's career suggest about politicians and the media?

- Boothby was able to use his money and contacts to protect himself from damaging media coverage.
- Until the mid-1960s, the press was restrained and nervous regarding the personal affairs of the rich and famous. Despite the indiscretions of Boothy and Dorothy Macmillan, the affair was kept secret.
- Without compelling evidence, newspapers were wary of publishing scandalous material. The *Mirror*'s payment of huge damages to Boothby served as a serious deterrent to other editors.

Boothby's successful management of the media contrasts sharply with his political successors. In the 1980s and 1990s the careers of Jeffrey Archer, David Mellor and Paddy Ashdown were devastated by media coverage of their sexual affairs. Powerful connections and a healthy bank balance could not stop tabloid exposure of their private lives nor protect their political futures.

A closer look at newspapers: a case study of the Profumo affair

Newspapers are invaluable sources of information for historians. But they are also highly complex and diverse. It is well worth investing a bit of time to find out about a particular newspaper before using it as evidence in your writing.

Funding
Some papers are free and funded entirely through advertising. Most papers rely very heavily on advertising for revenues (70 per cent or more of their funds). This means newspaper editors have to pay attention to the views of their advertisers.

Political stance
Unlike the television media, papers usually adopt a political viewpoint, e.g. most readers of the *Daily Mail* are Conservative, those reading *The Guardian* are Liberal or Labour voters.

Circulation
Some newspapers, like the *Sun*, are mass market, with several million daily readers; others, like the quality paper *The Times*, have had less than half a million readers for most of the last 40 years.

Key features of newspapers to consider

Kind
Papers can be daily, evening or weekly and they may cater for local or national readers. The *Evening Standard* is an evening paper for those in the London area, for instance.

Class
Newspapers like *The Sun* have a large working-class readership while *The Times* and *The Telegraph* are generally read by the better off. *The Times* prides itself on being read by the 'political elite'.

Style
Tabloid papers like the *Daily Mirror* are smaller and fatter with larger pictures and bold headlines. Broadsheet newspapers like the *Daily Telegraph* are much wider and thinner with more text and smaller type.

The type of newspaper greatly affects how major news stories are reported. When the Profumo affair broke, this is how it was reported in two leading newspapers:

Page 12, *The Times*, 6 June 1963

'Mr Profumo resigns: I misled the House'

The Times placed its main news items in the centre of the paper and had advertisements on the front page. Nevertheless its coverage of the Profumo affair was very low key with no photographs and simple factual headlines.

Front page, *Daily Mirror*, 6 June 1963

'Profumo Quits'

The *Mirror* used large headlines, two photographs and varied typefaces in its full-page treatment of the affair. Strong language was used in the news report: the affair was a 'political sensation', Profumo's career was 'in ruins' and his letter was 'dramatic'. Contrast this with the neutral language of *The Times* report on the same day.

Even within newspapers there are different kinds of writing by different writers for different purposes. Study the following three examples of coverage of the Profumo affair by *The Times* newspaper.

Example 1: 6 June 1963 News report

Written by the Political Correspondent
Purpose: Factual account of the main events. Even in this form of writing the choice of language and headings can reveal the angle or slant of the report. The report was under three headings:

- Mr Profumo resigns: I misled the House
- Denial of impropriety not true
- 'Grave misdemeanour' to protect wife and family

Admitting that he was 'guilty of a grave misdemeanour' in deceiving the House of Commons about the nature of his associations with the witness who disappeared – Miss Christine Keeler, a model, aged 21 – Mr John Profumo, Secretary of State for War, has resigned his office and his seat in the Commons.

His resignation comes partly as a consequence of representations made to the Prime Minister and the Home Secretary by Dr Stephen Ward, an osteopath, at whose flat Mr Profumo met Miss Keeler on several occasions.

Example 2: 11 June 1963 Editorial

Written by the editor of *The Times*
In this part of the newspaper, the editor offers his opinions on some of the leading news stories in the paper. Normally his views would be expected to broadly reflect those of his readers although sometimes editorials can mould or challenge their readers' opinions. Below is an extract from a long editorial on the Profumo affair where the editor comments on Labour leader Harold Wilson's emphasis on security rather than morality. Most readers of *The Times* were Conservatives and as the Profumo scandal weakened the Tory party, an attack on the Labour leader was likely to be popular.

It *is* a moral issue

Mr Harold Wilson also [as well as Macmillan] is a shrewd politician and his immediate reaction was to stress that Labour's concern was about security, not about morals. (It will be interesting to see how he can deploy his attack on the Government's security arrangements without the question of Mr Profumo's morals coming in.) Everyone has been so busy assuring the public that the affair is not one of morals, that it is time to assert that it is. Morals have been discounted too long. A judge may be justified in reminding a jury 'This is not a court of morals'. The same exemption cannot be allowed public opinion, without rot setting in and all standards suffering in the long run. The British are not by and large an immoral nation but through their pathetic fear of being called smug they make themselves out to be one.

Example 3: 15 June 1963 Letter to the Editor

There was great competition to get letters published in such a distinguished paper as *The Times* and the editor himself commented that he received more correspondence on this issue than any other. Letter writers wanted the chance to influence opinion, to share their knowledge and enjoy the prestige of having their views printed. How did the editor select which to publish? The editor would take into account the quality of the writing and the expertise and status of the writer. He would also aim to publish a range of letters which would broadly reflect the balance of the views expressed. On this date he wrote a note under a letter supporting his editorial stating that 'many similar letters have been received'. The letter below expresses the political concerns of many Conservatives about the unfolding crisis:

Sir, There is a great deal of profound and no doubt sincere opinion expressed in your correspondence columns today but I consider that the greatest injustice arising from the Profumo affair has not been sufficiently stressed i.e. that this defection has any connexion whatsoever with Conservatism.

The fact that Mr Profumo was a Conservative is quite incidental: no doubt there have been and perhaps are many more sordid cases in the Labour ranks if we cared to look for them. Indeed there was recently exposed a much worse case morally in the Labour Party than the one being discussed so widely at the moment. I refer to a very unpleasant homosexual case, than which surely nothing can be lower, but I did not notice that the Labour Party was castigated on account of this.

The real danger of this implied connexion between moral defection and Conservatism is that a lot of misguided people might be persuaded to vote for the Labour Party under the influence of the publicity being given to the Profumo case and one shudders to think of the effect a Labour Government could have during these difficult times …

Yours faithfully
C Stuart Dobson
Stoke on Trent

Key pointers for using newspapers

- **The kind of newspaper:** With its conservative, middle-class readership, *The Times* provides useful insight into the reactions of the political and social elite. Their preoccupations were political and moral and the coverage of the issue was serious in tone. As most of their readers were Conservative supporters, *The Times* focused on Profumo's lapses as an individual, not weaknesses in the Conservative government or social elites.

  By contrast, tabloid newspapers gave their readers many titillating details of the affair, satirical cartoons and large photos of the key figures. The events were seen as an opportunity to expose misbehaviour and mistakes made by many establishment figures and weaknesses in Conservative rule.

- **The form of newspaper writing:** A newspaper is a collaborative work of teams of journalists with different expertise. While news reports may be mostly factual, the editorial reveals the paper's political stance. Although selected from a large pool, letters from the public provide a flavour of readers' attitudes.

  It is safe to say that most readers of *The Times* shared the moral outrage expressed in the editorial. Both the editor and most of the letter writers shared the assumption that the social and political elites should set an example to the rest of society. There was concern that the Profumo affair would undermine this position of moral leadership.

  In the popular press, the satirical and mocking coverage of the affair suggests that these assumptions were already out of date.

This study of newspaper coverage of the Profumo affair is a strong reminder of the dangers of generalisations. The tone and content of *The Times*' reporting of the affair reflects the concerns of the privileged classes. But this is only a small part of the story. To understand how the affair transformed the attitudes of press and public to their so-called social superiors, you would need to turn to the mass circulation tabloids.

Conclusion

When I drive to work in the morning, I pass the children arriving at the local primary school for their day's lessons. Some walk, some cycle, many are dropped off by car. Accompanied by mums, dads or childminders, they wear sensible, machine-washable uniforms and carry colourful lunch boxes. Their faces reflect the multi-racial nature of modern Britain. Inside school, girls and boys learn together and both use computers with confidence and skill. Most seem very happy to skip through the school gates.

Their school days will be very different from my own in the 1960s. Kitted out in shirt, tie, felt hat and box-pleat tunic, my sisters and I walked to school on our own, whatever the weather. The school day started with a religious assembly with hymn and prayers. Learning to write involved an inkwell, dip pen and copy books. Sewing and knitting figured strongly in the timetable. School meals were compulsory, hot and usually disgusting. My school mates were all white and there was only one girl in my class whose parents were divorced. There were a lot of tellings-off: dirty nails and poor handwriting were my main offences. School days were very different then.

These changes in schooling reflect the transformation of British society which has occurred in the last sixty years. Many changes are positive. The British have become healthier and wealthier. Most of us go on foreign holidays, live in centrally heated homes and own our own cars. The nation is certainly more mixed than it was – neighbourhood mosques have mostly been accepted and Asian takeaway food warmly embraced. Social attitudes have become more relaxed, with pre-marital sex, homosexuality and divorce no longer frowned upon in general society. Dads are now often at the heart of British families; not just the breadwinners and disciplinarians. Institutions such as the Church of England or the police force are not automatically respected but held up to scrutiny. In some ways Britain has become a kinder and more tolerant place to live.

Yet it is not an entirely rosy picture. British families seem now to be more fearful than ever before. Fewer children walk to school, play outside or climb trees. Fear of crime and terrorism has led to more suspicion of foreigners or strangers. Decline in religious belief has been accompanied by growing consumerism, with shops rather than churches dominating British Sundays. A minority of British children spend their whole childhood living with their mum and dad in a single household. Many in the older generation regret the loss of family cohesion, community spirit and respect for authority that they associate with earlier decades. Nor has Britain become a more equal society. The chances of someone from the working class becoming a judge, a brain surgeon or a politician are no greater now than they were in 1950. Life expectancy in Britain's poorest

Political parties in power	Prime ministers	Key phases of social change
1945–51 Labour	Clement Attlee	**Labour's welfare state 1945–51** **Provision of state welfare from the 'cradle to the grave' such as:** National Insurance and National Assistance; National Health Service; Housing Acts; National Health Service.
1951–64 Conservative	Winston Churchill Anthony Eden Harold Macmillan Alec Douglas Home	
1964–70 Labour	Harold Wilson	**Labour and 'The Liberal Hour' 1964–70** **Wilson's government passed a series of laws liberalising British society:** Homosexuality decriminalised; divorce laws reformed; abortion legalised; equal pay introduced; contraception made available on the NHS; censorship relaxed; expansion of the universities; laws passed to improve race relations.
1970–74 Conservative	Edward Heath	**The Thatcher era 1979–97** **Thatcher passed a series of measures to control inflation and encourage independence and efficiency:** Cuts in public spending on health and education; Housing Act passed allowing council tenants to buy their houses; immigration was restricted further; Sunday trading was permitted.
1974–79 Labour	Harold Wilson James Callaghan	
1979–97 Conservative	Margaret Thatcher John Major	**Blair and 'New Labour' 1997–2005** **A mix of social reform and spending and measures to make welfare affordable:** Generous public spending on schools and hospitals (much based on public/private partnerships); national minimum wage established; civil partnerships introduced.
1997–2005 Labour	Tony Blair	

Key trends

British family life
In the 1940s the two-parent nuclear family was the norm, with the man as the main breadwinner. By the 1990s one-third of births were outside of marriage and by 2000 a quarter of British families were headed by a single parent.

Expansion of education
Free secondary education to the age of 15 had been introduced in the 1940s (raised again to 16 in 1973). Wilson's government greatly expanded university education. By 2000 there were ten times as many students in higher education than there had been in 1954.

Multi-culturalism and secularisation
Britain has become a multi-faith, multi-racial society, with growing numbers of non-Christian believers, especially Muslims. Christian belief and church-going have steadily declined – only 13% of Britons in 2000 belonged to a Christian church. Asian and Caribbean immigration has been followed by increasing numbers of migrants from Eastern Europe.

The rise in living standards and consumerism
Between 1945 and 2000 the real income of British families increased threefold. Alongside rising home ownership, there was a massive increase in TV and car ownership and consumption of household goods.

While in the early 1950s less than half of British households had a television or fridge, by the late 1990s, 99% had them.

Better health, longer lives
Medical advances and improved diet, housing and lifestyle have led to a massive rise in life expectancy and the population is becoming older. In 1900 less than 5% of the population was over 65: by 2000 this was over 16%. This has placed a much greater burden on welfare and health services.

Spotlight on

Family Allowances Act 1945
This was a regular payment for second and subsequent children, paid to the mother. It raised family incomes by as much as 10% when it was first introduced in 1946.

1962 Education Act and the Robbins Report
This required local education authorities to provide grants to support students in higher education. The Robbins report led to the massive expansion of higher education.

△ Roy Jenkins, responsible for several liberal laws introduced in the 1960s.

Broadcasting Act 1990
This deregulated television broadcasting, opening the way to cable and satellite television and the option of multiple channels.

Sunday Trading Act 1994
This allowed shops to open on Sundays despite a strong campaign from those determined to 'keep Sunday special'. Although opening hours were restricted, Sunday shopping quickly became an established habit.

Private Finance Initiative and public/private partnerships
These involved using private companies to fund building and infrastructure projects in health, transport and education. Although the Labour party had initially opposed this conservative model, once in power they adopted it as the only affordable way of improving buildings and infrastructure.

communities is more than 20 years below the national average. The age of affluence and technology has brought its own health problems too, such as binge drinking and obesity. Sadly, higher living standards have not made Britain a happier nation. Mental health problems, such as depression and addictions, have increased in the last sixty years.

So British society has changed in many fundamental ways since 1945. How good or bad or how extensive these changes have been varies according to viewpoint and circumstances. For some groups, such as homosexuals and working women, the changes have been major and largely positive. The lives of the homeless or rural farmers, however, have changed much less. It is also important to recognise that social change has been neither constant nor predictable. Twentieth-century predictions of the ending of the British monarchy were frequent, as it appeared to be an outdated symbol of privilege and empire, well past its sell-by date. Yet it has proved to be a remarkably resilient institution. The queen's popularity ratings have remained the envy of most of the prime ministers who have served under her in her sixty-year reign. New technologies, it was thought, would replace the old, yet the advent of television did not lead to the death of radio and cinema after all. While there has been a steady liberalisation of sexual attitudes over the past sixty years, the importance of the family unit has remained paramount.

British society in 2005 and beyond retains some of the features of Britain in 1945. We still eat fish and chips as well as Chinese take-aways. We still celebrate Guy Fawkes Night but we enjoy the Notting Hill Carnival too. Sunday roast dinners remain a British tradition, but for most, church-going does not. British businessmen have lost their bowler hats but still retain their ties. Parents share childcare but, in most homes, it's still women who do the laundry. The pub, the bingo hall and the football stadium are enduring parts of British social life but are now supplemented by multiplex cinemas and pizza restaurants. British society has evolved in the last sixty years, but just as you can recognise the same family features in a grandparent and a grandchild, so you can see the Britain of 1945 in the Britain of sixty years later.

Index

Headings in **bold** refer to glossary terms.